SMALL WONDERS: YEAR-ROUND-ALASKA

written by Mary Shields   illustrated by Nancy van Veenan

pyrola publishing
p.o. box 80961 fairbanks alaska 99708

Also by Mary Shields and Nancy van Veenen and available from Pyrola Publishing:

This-Year-Round-Alaska Wall Journal, Pyrola Publishing, 1986.
    18" Full color reproduction of the cover of this book.
    Suitable for framing or to use for your own nature notes.

Sled Dog Trails, Alaska Northwest Publishing Co. 1984.

Acknowledgements

I thank the following people for their help, patience, encouragement, criticism and friendship:
Jim Anderson, Mary Bishop, Chris Brann—Dragon Press, John Manthei,
Kathy Pearse—Ptarmigan Typing, Leah Shields, Connie Taylor—Fathom Graphics,
Nancy van Veenen and John Wright.

From The Complete Poems of Carl Sandburg, copyright 1950 by Carl Sandburg;
renewed 1978 by Margaret Sandburg, Helga Sandburg Crile and Janet Sandburg.
Reprinted by permission of Hartcourt Brace Jovanovich, Inc.

Excerpts from "Seeing" in Pilgrim at Tinker Creek by Annie Dillard copyright © 1974 by Annie Dillard.
Reprinted by permission of Harper and Row Publishers.

First Printing   April 1987

ISBN 0-9618348-0-3

Typeset by Fathom Graphics, Cordova, Alaska
Printed by Dragon Press, Delta Junction, Alaska
Printed in the United States of America

pyrola publishing
Box 80961, Fairbanks, Alaska 99708

Dedicated to the
black-capped and boreal chickadees —
small wonders that sing even at 40° below zero.

Table of Contents

Introduction

Introduction

Alaska is a vast wonderland. The immense snows quiet the endless mountain ranges and melt slowly into the wide, meandering rivers. The rivers carve their paths through the forests to the seas to join the great tides heaving to the other side of the world.

Sometimes Alaska is overwhelming. There is more than a visitor can see in an entire summer's vacation, more than a sourdough can experience in a hundred lifetimes. So, to begin my understanding, I look for small wonders and simple gifts close around me. They are everywhere.

The closer I look, the more there is to see. I see not only the miniature miracles occurring each day, but also the invisible intertwinings that stretch between them. I'm beginning to understand the relationships between things: the gossamer threads of the web of life — that web of life seen only while looking into the sun.

I've made a special calendar to help put the small wonders in their place. My calendar is round like a spider's web, round like a many-petaled flower. The months and seasons radiate out from the sun which holds the center. Rays shoot out of the sun denoting Summer Solstice, Winter Solstice, Spring Equinox, and Fall Equinox. I add notes for leaf-out, leaf-drop, breakup, and freeze-up, the northward migration of geese and their southerly return, and more and more and more. There is no beginning, no end.

Over the years I have added more notes to my calendars, and now I think of them as Wall Journals. With more notes come more understandings. By looking for those small wonders, I am becoming more intimately aware of how life responds to the roll of the earth around the sun. I find a great joy in these simple observations of the natural world and the recognition and acceptance of my own place in this world.

Please, Dear Reader, read on. Share my wonderings of 14 years on a particular patch of earth, in a valley 30 miles west of Fairbanks. *You may want to begin reading in the current month's chapter and take a full year to finish, month by month as they roll by.* As you read, go out and explore the world gathered around you. Be prepared to return with new delights in your heart, for the earth has endless surprises for those who come looking. Small wonders and simple gifts — they are everywhere.

April — Every Ending Marks A New Beginning

April 2, 24°   It is no use trying to stay inside. The past six months have been time enough to enjoy the warm, cozy cabin. Now my spirit demands being *out the door*, out into the windy forest.

Last night's freezing temperature captured the runaway runoff of yesterday afternoon, sealing its escape in the snow. Today's new crust is not quite strong enough to walk on, so I stay on my snowshoes — but not on the trails! My webbed feet seldom break through and I can go anywhere effortlessly; even my tracks can't keep up with me.

I start out quickly, aiming uphill through the forest to warm up. Out along the edge of the old burn, I stop to admire a first circle of spring. The snow is completely gone from a four-foot radius around the trunk of an old white spruce tree. The colors and smells of a season yet to come invite me to enter. I leave my snowshoes in their own world so I won't track in snow as I crawl in under the low branches. A comfortable spot in the crook of friendly roots welcomes me. I lean back against the trunk, inhaling the essence of spruce needles and pitch. This soft cushion of needles has been accumulating throughout the life of the tree. A layer sifted down over 100 years ago when the United States bought Alaska from the Russians. Perhaps layers were even sifting down when Peter the Great first sent Vitus Bering to explore the North Pacific over 250 years ago.

This tree survived the most recent wildfire 30 years ago and is probably the parent tree of these hundreds of saplings growing up in the tree's revolving shadow. For at least 200 years these bountiful branches have bounced down the winter's snowfalls, piling up the accumulations around the edge of this circle. In this country, Interior Alaska, wildfire usually burns every 100 years, so this sanctuary of over 200-year-old forest is rare and precious.

1

Red squirrels have tunneled down through the needles and spruce cones, and the remains of squirrels' mossy nests still nestle in the branches above. Leftovers from recent squirrel picnics pile up neatly on the exposed roots. The bracts, or petals, of the cones have been snipped off and the small white seeds have been eaten. Only a tuft of bracts remains at the end of each empty cone core, forming a brown bloom on a three-inch stem. My young friend Maia Wright split open some of these stripped cones and found moth larvae overwintering there.

I weave this winter flower into my braid, to carry home and tuck into a crack in the log wall, to remember this small wonder under the old spruce tree.

Farther out from the trunk, but still under the umbrella of branches, native grasses have pushed up through the needles. The dry golden leaves and stems seem so foreign to my eyes, now accustomed to winter's white. Beyond the dead grass, curls and feathers of brilliant green moss startle my senses. Again I am surprised to feel each plume frozen in its delicate, graceful uprising. Soon the crystal spell will end, and the green growth will begin. April is like that. April is a give-and-take between winter and spring. The circle around this tree is merely a hole in the great white blanket which still covers the earth. Winter will give in during the weeks to come and spring will take the circles around all these trees and enlarge them into bright brown and green patches in the white blanket. Perhaps the red squirrels will stitch up the patches, as they skitter and chase each other in their wild race from tree to tree. Yes, squirrel tracks would be just the right topstitching for this grand forest quilt.

April 7, 14°   Fifth sunny day in a row! The winter birds seem to be celebrating their survival of another long, cold winter, celebrating with all their hearts and lungs. Now is a good time to appreciate their sourdough songs — now before the returning spring migrants overwhelm the forest with their exotic chorales. A merry band of redpolls, gregarious sparrow-size birds, swoops over the alders along the creek while I fill the water pails this afternoon. One robust bird lands in the branches above me and sings out his repertoire. The entire flock simultaneously alights as if all were connected by invisible threads. Another reckless redpoll lands on my head and perches there for half a minute. I hold my breath.

April 9, 12°   I proclaim today "Hairy Woodpecker Day"! Let there be woodpeckers! And there shall be, I'm sure of it. Last year on April 9th I was working out in the dog yard when I noticed Harriet, the female hairy woodpecker of this neighborhood, sitting on a long horizontal birch branch that stretched out over the cabin. This seemed an odd place for her, as woodpeckers usually land against the trunks of trees and work their way up and down, holding a vertical position, their stiff tail feathers supporting them. Most woodpeckers have four toes on each foot, with two toes pointing forward and two pointing backward, excellent foot gear for their tree climbing, but not for perching.

   As I was watching Harriet sitting on the branch, I heard Harry, the male woodpecker, rattling in through the woods toward the cabin. The handsome black-and-white bird, with the dramatic red topknot, cruised in and landed on the birch branch holding Harriet, about six feet away. Slowly he scrambled toward the female, moving clumsily along the branch. Closer and closer, and then suddenly he jumped on her back and mounted her. The breeding lasted for about a minute, and then Harry swooped off, racketing his way through the woods. Harriet remained motionless for about five minutes and then she also whisked off through the trees.

   To witness this intimate behavior was a surprise. But now I must tell you something even more surprising. Today, exactly one year later, again on April 9th, again on the very same birch branch, a second hairy woodpecker breeding took place.

April 10, 20°   The gray jays are extremely active again. Now five jays visit the feeder, while all winter only three were present. Lots of chasing around and singing; I wish I was certain about who's who. Occasionally one of the jay's delicate body feathers floats down to the snow. The dark charcoal feathers absorb the solar heat and melt about half an inch into the snow.

   The boreal owls also join the avian chorus. Their quavering, hollow calls go on for minutes without a stop for catching a breath, all day long and all the night too. The quiet of the winter forest has ended and spring's crescendo is beginning.

April 12, 27°   The snow has compacted considerably in the last week. This has happened by the restructuring and reorientation of the crystals along with sublimation, or the change from a solid to a gas without being a liquid. The brown and green circles surrounding trees have joined to form stripes along the ridgetops and knolls. Looking toward the south-facing hills, 50 percent of the land is dark and snow free. Looking out across the valley, toward the north-facing slopes, all is still white and black-spruce green. Bears are content in their dens up there. For a while longer I'll still need my snowshoes if I want to venture very far.

April 19, 15°   6 a.m. The sun is slicing in between the tree trunks by 4 a.m. As the sky glows a luminous blue, I find sleeping past 5:30 impossible. The winds swirl down the valley, swaying the tall spruce trees and my eager spirit, with a wanderlust born in the mountains. This early in the day the crust is still frozen hard and the cold winds maintain the trails. I harness the dogs to make one last dash up to my winter retreat, high on the ridgetop. The trail is smooth and fast. I leave the team tied off at treeline and climb up into the rocks for a farewell look out over the snowy land. The bright rock lichens, orange, yellow, black, and brown, delight my winter eyes. Wedged in between the dark crags, I imagine some radiant warmth trapped there, but the unrelenting wind steals away my fantasy. After only ten minutes I am freezing from the wind and must surrender and retreat.

   Just then I hear them! Throwing back my hood, yanking off my scarf, I strain my eyes, strain my ears, and then, yes . . . I hear them again. There against the pure blue sky, an ever-changing, wobbly V of

geese pushes west into the wind. The wild geese have returned! Their urgent cries echo their desire to reach the summer nesting grounds.

"Welcome home!" I shout up to them, but my greeting is intercepted by the wind. I return down-valley with the dog team, the refrain of goose music in my ears. Nothing is quite the same anymore.

The trail home is slushy and every depression is deep with brown water. The return trip is a slow one. Nothing is quite the same anymore, once the wild geese have returned. April is like that.

April 27, 30°   Oh, if the morning could only last all day long! There is so much to keep an eye on. Anticipation blows in with the waking wind. So do the mosquitoes, the big slow ones that overwinter as adults. Over half of their body weight is composed of alcohols and glycols, which serve as antifreeze and allow them out this early. Down by the creek I spy the first lavender moths and their cousins the mourning cloak butterflies.

Varied thrushes are the first songbirds to arrive. They ring here . . . there . . . and then, over there. A friend calls them the "telephone" birds because they sound like telephones ringing, each on a different note. For the first few days here, the varied thrushes' rings are weak and infrequent. Once they rest up from the long flight and settle in, the tempo picks up. I certainly don't mind a few mosquitoes if they are the prerequisite for songbirds, and each year I marvel at their timing.

Incredibly pure-white swans race over, sounding like barking dogs as they move up the valley. A skein of about 20 geese skims under the low clouds, just over the treetops. I hear their wings fanning the air. No matter how often I see them, I always drop everything and admire the wonder of geese.

No sandhill cranes yet, but I know they must be close. My husband John and I eat lunch out under the big spruce in front of the cabin, despite John's insistence that "it is too early and too cold out there." We often hear our first cranes while having a picnic out under that tree. I just want to be ready.

John is a good sport about my goose celebrations. Last night we slept rather coldly, our big corduroy-covered quilt gathered close around us. Why coldly? Because we carried the bed outside and set it down on the end of the knoll in front of the cabin. The lower legs were leveled with firewood, and we fell asleep under the stars and hopefully under wild wings. Alas, we didn't hear any geese, and we were cold. The sleeping bags were way up in the high cache, so we just shivered together under the quilt. Waking up in a big bed in the middle of a spring forest is like waking up in a fairy tale. Prince Charming smiled back a silly grin to confirm the dream was reality.

Three juncos, the first to return this year, hop around under the bird feeder. They could have a feast up on the feeder, but they always prefer scratching around on the ground. The gray jays only come once or twice a day now. They are very secretive and a little nervous. No doubt the babies have hatched.

April 29, 36°   The willows shooting up through the five feet of overflow ice on the creek hold plump, colorful buds, just ready to open. Willows like these with big silky buds are called pussywillows. Along the arched stems, the buds perch like a row of red-birds, each erect and facing the sun. Once the buds open out into catkins, I need to return daily if I want to see all the bright explosions of pollen. As the overflow melts, so will my eye-level view. In two weeks I'll be looking up three feet at the catkins.

April 30, 35°   Walked four miles down the trail, no snowshoes needed! Feels so good and light and free. A line of wolf tracks is frozen in the creek slush. That's why the dogs were howling last night — just a long-lost cousin. One wolf, trotting along in the night, eyes, ears, and nose alert. Does the wolf share my exhilaration over such easy walking?

Puddles have melted out around various dark objects which have absorbed the radiant solar heat. Through the water the vegetation looks magnified, drops acting as converging lenses, enlarging the images. Last autumn's leaves and the bright leafy lichens are worthy of close examination through these round, liquid magnifying glasses. From the raven's-eye view, if that rakish fellow ever looks down as he twirl-dives after his companion, perhaps all these sparkling puddles look like decorative buttons, tucked in here and there on the dark crazy-quilt now covering the earth. Only small white patches remain. Winter's dark sky and light ground is reversing toward summer's light sky and dark ground. April is like that: Every ending marks a new beginning.

May — In the Beginning...

May 2, 40°   In the beginning there is *Equisetum* — horsetail — a herd of wild horsetails, a stampede of young stallions restless from the long winter. They first appear as dull olive, almost translucent nubs, camouflaged well with the forest floor. After I discover one plant, I immediately see thousands of others. They return from ancient root systems, year after year after year, secretly pushing up through the dead leaves. Often the new stems poke up through leaves, carrying them four or five inches into the air in a burst of growth. Within weeks, tiers of needle-thin, wispy leaves will radiate out in sprays of pale green, at even vertical intervals. How these delicate swirls must tickle the nose of a snowshoe hare resting there, contemplating the return of the green world of its winter dreams.

Evolutionarily, horsetails are one of the most primitive plants in the Interior. As they were the first to come in the beginning of plants, they are the first to come in the beginning of spring. In August they are the first plants to die off, usually nipped by the first frost-bites of beginning autumn.

May 5, 44°   John brings in nine gallons of birch sap collected from five trees during the past 12 hours. I swirl the brew with the long-handled paddle in the big cauldron, which is simmering over the outside fire. The aromatic steam rises to join the sweet smoke from the punky birch fire below and swirls out through the woods. The smoke curls here and there, feeling for just the right path through the trees. The fragrance must tempt every black bear with a sweet-tooth, and that may be every black bear. I can't resist either and take a sip to see if the concentrate is distilled enough. "Patience, Mary!" I remind myself. "Birch syrup takes a long time a-brewing." Only one gallon of the final ambrosia is created out of 40 gallons of birch sap.

May 7, 52°   Under the trees in the old forest the wintergreens are celebrating their days in the sun. During these last quick weeks before leaf-out, the sunlight pours in through the bare branches, flooding the forest floor, which lives mostly in shade the rest of the summer. The wintergreens — the pyrolas, low-bush cranberries, Labrador tea, and twin flowers — are ready and waving their old leaves at the sun. Their lush dark green delights my eyes, testifying to life outlasting the dark beneath the long winter's snow.

And even below the wintergreens, the mosses observe their birthdays. The recent snow melt saturated their minute leaves, activating every cell to produce chlorophyll. This brilliant green, the first growth of this year, begins to add another layer to the old plants. I carefully part the moss, reach down, and try to pluck out a single plant, entire with its roots. Impossible — the moss goes on forever. I lift up what I can reach and examine it closely. Every half inch a horizontal feather springs out, making the moss look like a tiny staircase. Each step marks a year's growth. How many years remain in the lower part, still attached to the roots? I snuggle the green marvel back in amongst its kin, wishing it might continue to grow, but knowing I have sacrificed this one for my own curiosity. The plant will decompose and nourish the others. Happy Birthdays, feather moss.

The grass has burst up two inches high. Down by the creek a small band of coltsfoot appears. Any day the small yellow violets will be up. Incredibly tiny fireweed shoots explode out of the ground like miniature fireworks — a display that will repeat itself with each developmental stage of this plant throughout the summer. Those first green and red outbursts will grow half an inch a day, with the tallest plants reaching up to six feet by September.

A profusion of fuchsia-colored blossoms will flare up the stem from the bottom to top, a chain reaction of petals, stigmas, and anthers, taking the entire summer to reach the highest tip. We say that summer is over when the fireweed blooms to the top, and this adage proves consistently true.

The next fireweed explosion comes with the bursting of the long, slender seedpods which rupture along four symmetrical seams, expelling millions of airborne seeds. The seeds drift off in search of soil on delicate white whispy rotors. Next the leaves flare out in maroon with blazes of red and green. Yes, _fireworks_ would be a truer descriptive name for fireweed.

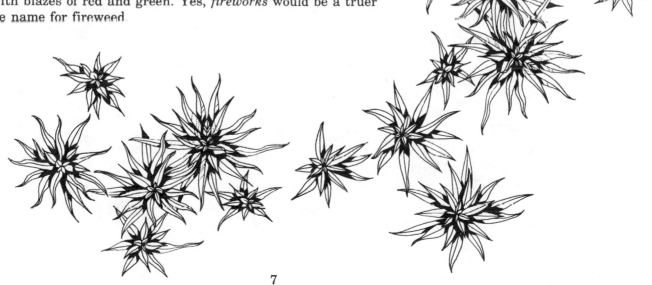

May 10, 50°   Windy, windy! Today wins the "Best Day of the Spring Award" by unanimous consent. High winds swoosh through the forest, teasing the cautious buds to shake out their leaves.

John and I work on future years' firewood supply, harvesting the birch trees that have blown over during the winter. John saws the trunks into stove lengths and then splits them with the maul into quarters or eighths, depending on the size of the round. The sweet smell of the sap thickens the air, intoxicating us, intensifying our spring fever. I stack the pieces with the bark side up, in rows between two standing trees. I attempt to make stable, aesthetically pleasing woodpiles, as I will visit them on my winter walks, remembering these sweet spring days. There is a satisfying beauty in the patterns that appear in a woodpile, both for the lines of the wood and the security of knowing there will be a warm cabin in the cold winters to come. Next winter I will dogsled the wood back to the woodshed, for a second year of air drying. By letting the wood dry for at least two years, we will get the most out of the logs and conserve our resource.

I place scraps of birch bark over the woodpile to keep out the rain and stand back to admire the neat pattern of wood. Now what do the black bears of summer think when they stumble into these piles in their wanderings?

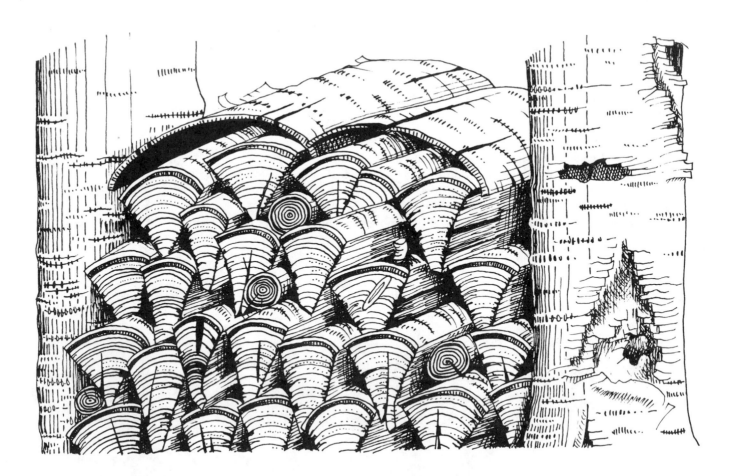

May 11, 49°   Now you see them, in two weeks you won't. Now, before the shadows' confusion and camouflage of leaf-out, the small birds are easily seen. I go out early — never early enough — but early. The temperature is still around freezing at 6 a.m. Juncos, sparrows, warblers, kinglets, and thrushes dominate the forest. I hesitate to add my own rough song. Years ago I read, "A bird doesn't sing because he has an answer, a bird sings because he has a song." I don't remember where I read it, but I like it. So I sing softly today, humbled by the clear notes ringing through the forest.

May 12, 53°   The chickadees are stealing dog fur from the dog yard where the sled dogs are beginning to shake off the underfur of winter. The chickadees pack their bills with this fallout of fleece and flit, flit, flit off to their secret nesting trees. A full-grown chickadee weighs less than half an ounce. How small can a baby chickadee be?

May 13, 52°   Now the alders take their turn in the sun. Alders are common, perhaps the most common shrub in the Interior of Alaska. They're everywhere. If you try to travel cross-country, alders are always in your way. But for the next two weeks, the humble alder will win my attention.

Alders, the last to leaf out, are the next after willows to make flowers. Unlike willows, both the male and female flowers are on the same plant. The male catkins opened late in April, forming two- to three-inch dangling chains of blossoms, each reddish-yellow flower forming a platelet of the whole. After about two weeks of warm weather, the pollen is on the wind with perfect timing, for the female catkins (which will grow to be the winter cones) are then ripening, opening to catch the pollen. In another week the leaf buds break, and the two perfect deep-green leaves quietly, gracefully, bend back away from each other. The elongated leaves are tightly pleated lengthwise in the bud, and as they spread apart from each other, the leaves unfold in perfect symmetry. And this is the part that I love to watch, the leaves reaching out until they find their own private space in the sun, a space not shaded by any other leaf. After the twin leaves radiate out this way, a third leaf sprouts on a new stem, stretching, ever so slowly, off toward its own place in the sun. By the time this third leaf is opening, all the other trees and shrubs are well into the green glory. The alder moves slowly at first, but this careful spacing pays off, and by the end of summer, the alder's growth will surpass all except some reckless willows. When entire trunks are cut down or destroyed, alders send up hardy sucker shoots, growing rapidly from the original root system. No wonder they are everywhere. Alders try harder!

May 14, 52°   Breakup in Alaska is a most special ritual of spring. The high sun teases the temperature and the winter snows begin their long, downhill journey to the sea. The sun is officially up about 2:30 a.m. and sets around 9 p.m. Only a few faint stars left. No more darkness.

Each evening we walk down to the creek to see how breakup is progressing. We have our own little tripod to mark the official moment of ice movement, but usually the tripod just eases down into the melting overflow ice. (Not quite as exciting as the big tripod in Nenana, where thousands of dollars go to the lucky winners when the ice moves enough to break the string connecting it to the shore.)

I hear the song of the restless water growing all day. In the morning the trickle is gentle and soothing. By afternoon a steady crescendo builds, and by evening the grand finale roars in celebration of the wanderlust of snowy waters.

Our creek is only a foot wide in summer. The spring gurgles up out of the ground about a half mile up the valley. All winter long, the water burbled up, freezing into overflow ice, which now spreads some 15 feet wide and, burble by burble, has accumulated to a depth of seven feet. Runoff from the hills now roars down, cutting several deep channels in this ice. The water is tinted a deep rusty brown by tannic acid in the vegetation, which the runoff flows through. A free cup of herb tea with every cup of water! Great mounds of foam gather at the bends in the creek and on the log jams.

For a week now, breakup has marooned me on this island of upland forest. The dog trails in both directions are under water for miles. But this restless creek takes my mind downstream. I can flow with the flow down to Goldstream Creek and then west to Minto Flats. As the water meanders its way through the marshes and lakes, thousands of ducks and geese will fly over, some landing on the water to rest before continuing north to their breeding grounds. Goldstream Creek tumbles into the Chatanika River, which in turn, swirls into the Tolovana, which in more turns roars into the icy waters of the Tanana. The momentum of all that grinding ice and surging water overwhelms everything in its path. Gravel bars are swept clean, leaning trees are snapped off, and huge chunks of bank are undercut and carried away.

Downstream 150 miles our little creek, now a part of the Tanana River, joins the mighty Yukon. Villagers check their fishwheels and riverboats, secured to the bank last fall. Lowlanders prepare for possible flooding. Oldtimers sit on the bank listening and watching and waiting. When news comes that the ice has moved upstream, the whole village comes out to watch the greatest watershow on earth. Sometimes moose are caught midstream when the ice breaks. They drift by, teetering on the undulating ice floes. Few of these moose ever reach shore again.

Breakup continues on down the Yukon, closing out the winter trails and opening up the waterways of summer. In a month's time the water in our little creek will flow several thousand miles to the Bering Sea, to return again with the tide or the storm clouds of June. Perhaps this water will swirl past next summer's salmon, encouraging them to come home. Perhaps this very creek water will flow under the belly of a great bowhead whale!

No, I'm not marooned by breakup. This little creek takes me traveling.

May 16, 59°   There's a good joke going around in the woods these days. The rain has told it to the birds, and the birds never tire of repeating it over and over to the buds. At first the buds just snicker a bit . . . titter a little, chuckle quietly. Then a green giggle creeps out along the branches. After a few days (the rain repeating it, the birds repeating it) the buds cannot contain themselves any longer. They split open in chortles, guffaws, bellylaughs. In a week the trees are roaring out of control with laughing leaves. The hillsides bounce in a shimmering green. This joke is a great one, even though we all heard it just a year ago. I admire the earth's sense of humor.

The trees look so different with their leaves on again. My eye goes to the crown of leaves now, rather than the trunk and silhouette as in the preceding season. This new leaf green is the color of a promise fulfilled.

May 20, 50°   The jays have brought their babies to the picnic tree. The fluffy dark-charcoal young are nearly as large as their parents. How could they have gotten so big already? By eating constantly, I observe. That's all they seem to be interested in. They chase after their parents, landing below them in the branches, gaping their wide, white beaks, and quivering their wings, all with a desperate accompaniment of frantic squawking.

The sourdough jays respond in appropriate parenting manner, stuffing tidbits down into the babies' gullets, and at last the forest is quiet again. The adults glide down to my hand to inspect my offering. The jays aren't picky eaters. They make their living as scavengers, cleaning up the leftovers on the land. They have well earned their nickname, "camp robber."

The young jays won't land on my hand, but in time they'll follow the example of their parents and learn to trust me. I wonder if they'll enjoy the morning's leftover pancakes as much as I'll enjoy the grip of their thin talons and their light bundle of energy perched on my hand? Occasionally they "taste" my thumb, just to see if by any chance it has turned into something they can fly off with. The jays do seem to share a sense of humor with their cousins the ravens, notorious jokesters of the North.

So, the first young of the spring have made a visit. I welcome them with green greetings. The wide world awaits their sharp eyes and always adaptive ingenuity. Happy Birthday, clever baby jays.

May 22, 59°   More mosquitoes out now, scouting out the new year's prospects. They are easy to swat before they bite, and the worst thing about them is their warning of what is to soon come. Captain Jim of the Riverboat Discovery, a Fairbanks tour-boat, says "for every mosquito you kill, 10,000 survivors will come to the funeral!" But like them or not, they belong here as much as the rest of us.

3:30 a.m. The sled dogs bark that bark I know from experience means something is nearby . . . a bear? . . . a porcupine? I roll over and peer out of the window above the pillows. The dogs are looking straight back at me, and I lower my gaze to the bare ground under the window. The eaves extend over this ground, keeping the snow off, and there, two feet below me, sits a female spruce grouse, pecking away in the dirt, unconcerned with the eager dogs straining at the end of their chains. And then from around the corner of the woodshed, the male grouse sails in, thunders in with his heavy body landing only eight feet from the window, intent on impressing this female.

A miniature turkey, only one and a half pounds of bird, but with every feather puffed up and aquiver, he looks twice his normal size. His tail is fanned high behind him, in true turkey fashion, and the folds of crimson skin above each eye are erected to intensify their effect. With each step he fans his tail from side to side, making a dry, dusty, swishing sound which exaggerates this movement. When the male is within three feet of the female (and my window), he bends forward, closes his tail, begins to cluck softly, and then suddenly snaps open his tail feathers, erecting every single feather on his body, standing upright and appearing nearly twice his normal size!

With my face pressed to the window only two feet above the female grouse, I am getting the full effect of this display, and I am quite surprised and impressed. Alas, Ms. Grouse ignores his fancy strutting and continues pecking away in the dirt. Mr. Grouse is not dismayed. He repeats this expanding act again and again, to the delight of John, myself, and the sled dogs, all of whom are quite fascinated. I follow the grouse from window to window around the cabin, and after about half an hour, she sails off down the knoll with the male following her. The sled dogs go back to sleep and so do we, tickled to have witnessed a little of the more colorful life of our normally camouflaged neighbors.

May 23, 60°   Now they are all home and it's difficult to say one bird is more special than another. The bright warblers flashing yellow through the branches seem so exotic. The morning air rings with avian advertisements: "I am a white crown sparrow; I am a white crown sparrow," and the varied thrushes, the telephone birds, ringing over and over. The juncos juncoing around on the ground, fooling me with their variety of calls.

  But Nature is not to be taken for granted. Last night, after the air had hushed in the twilight, from way up in the corner of the old forest, one Swainson's thrush uttered its most incredible, most ethereal song. John heard it first. Then we waited very still, our mouths agape, our ears straining. And again, the thrush signaled the final arrival of the spring migration and cast a spell of perfection over the forest.

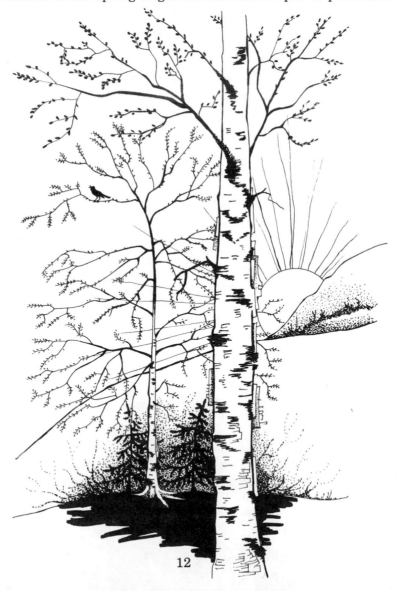

12

May 24, 64°   The larch, or as I prefer to call it, tamarack, is leafing out. I love to let "tam-a-rack" tumble off my tongue, bump out like my finger running along the branch, over the tiny volcanoes from which the needle-leaves erupt. The tamarack is the only deciduous tree in the North that grows needles instead of broad leaves. (Or is it the only coniferous tree that drops its needles?) The pale green needles are just pushing out today, and that freshest shade of green only lasts two to three days longer. I have been watching carefully to catch the color before it darkens to summer green. Each tiny bouquet of needles spreads out and goes about the business of growing. In another three and a half months, the needles will yellow and drift to the ground with the birch leaves. Again, the graceful silhouette of the tamarack will continue into winter, reminding me of the beauty of these green needles today.

May 25, 67°   The pussywillows are in full bloom, and from where I'm looking into the morning sun, the thicket along the creek reminds me of an orchard of apple trees, all in flower. The Interior hosts 17 different species of willows, with many hybrids to add to the confusion of identification. How do the moose ever tell them apart, for they certainly have their favorites?

I have studied the ragged stems left after many moose picnics, so rough compared to the smoothly clipped remains where hares have lunched. Using a plant key, I identified the species of willows and found three distinct favorites:

Salix pulchra, a short, bushy plant common in wet areas;

Salix arbusculoides, the tall, red-stemmed willow;

and *Salix alaxensis*, commonly called feltleaf willow after its velvety leaves.

All of these willows flourish in relatively early stages of plant succession, and these are just the areas moose call home. But I also find lots of moose sign in the old forest. Here, under the giant old aspens, little groves of saplings make their way up to the sun. More than half of these are snapped off about six feet high. Munching moose are responsible for this. They eat the tender young branches and move on — and there goes ten to 20 years of aspen growth. Does this pruning keep these aspen underlings in a constant stage of youth, easily accessible to moose? Or does it thin them out, allowing a few all the space and light they need to develop? Moose also gnaw the trunks of older aspen trees, leaving vertical gouges in the bark seven or eight feet up. If an elderly aspen crashes over, the bark will soon be stripped the length of the trunk, or at least that portion within reach of moose.

Next month when all the leaves are out, I will see if I can sense different smells from the different species. Of course, if I had a two-foot-long nose like a moose, the task would probably be much easier.

In the mud down by the creek crossing, I find a birth announcement this morning. The heavy, sharp, six-inch tracks of a cow moose are crossing the creek. And there, between her front and hind tracks, the delicate, light impressions of a brand-new calf are printed. The miniature replicates are less than two inches long, and they never stray far from the mother's big tracks.

I will keep my eyes open — with respect for new life and with concern for my own. I have stumbled into a cow with a new calf before, and I surprised myself at how fast I could climb a spindly, supposedly unclimbable, black spruce tree. I never even saw the calf, but it was the right time of year, late May, and the cow was most intent on keeping me out of a nearby willow thicket. She charged me four or five times, veering off at just the last minute as I waved my arms and screamed at her. After I scrambled up in the scrawny little spruce, she took out her anger on the trunk below me and nearby vegetation. I clung there for dear life, fascinated by my view of her from above, but not too certain how long the tree would hold me. The whole adventure was like a dream. I even enjoyed the humor of the scene, as if I was watching it happen to someone else.

After 20 minutes she disappeared into the willows and I eased myself slowly down the tree. Before I reached ground she was back, and I scurried up again to safety. After another 20 minutes all was quiet, and I eased down again. I returned in the direction I had come, making my way from climbable tree to climbable tree, my senses more alert than they had been in a long time.

May 27, 60°   Sitting on the little knoll above the creek, at the edge of the old burned forest, I enjoy an expansive view of sky. Shreds of birch bark rattle in the breeze, which is just enough wind to keep the bugs off. Above me in the blue, a snipe ascends with true determination and then suddenly dives straight down. The wind whistles through his tail, making a hollow, winnowing sound that follows him as he alternately dives and then climbs again. Perhaps a female will someday follow him, or at least be there waiting when he lands.

Toward sunset a few feeble croaks rise up from the wood frogs. Perhaps they have just eased up from the mud and leaves of hibernation. After a few more days of warmth, they will be fully revived and the croaking chorus will begin in earnest.

May 30, 62°   Out in the southwest corner of the forest, my eyes swing down to a small patch of bright fuchsia on the moss green. On hands and knees, I discover tiny four-inch-high orchids — the calypso orchids — almost gaudy, dancing in their lavender, purple, and bright yellow. From this vantage point their extremely sweet smell awakens my nose. The orchids seem so exotic, here in the boreal forest, but indeed they are a part. To discover a patch of orchids is like sharing a special secret with the forest, a privilege to be treasured. And this is only the beginning of the sun-days to come.

June — A Month of Sun-Days

June 3, 57°   The sudden explosion of quick, small mosquitoes keeps me moving. Hearing them buzz to a landing, feeling them exploring my skin, waiting for the attack; the anticipation is worse than the actual bite. It's incredible that these minute, bloodthirsty creatures can challenge the reasoning powers of my sophisticated brain, and win. They are good for my humility!

June 5, 62°   The first wildflowers are blooming today. The lavender-blue Jacob's ladder, the true-blue bluebells, and the wild-rose wild roses. To complement the bright petals, each flower perfumes the air with its own distinct fragrance. This flowering must be timed perfectly to coincide with the hatching of the pollinating insects. The profusion of plants in this area demonstrates great success in timing, for by August the seedpods are ripe. I have seen sparrows attack the Jacob's ladder pods, scattering the tiny seeds for several feet around the parent plant. No doubt some of the eaten seeds are not digested but are passed out by the birds later in the day. If those seeds happen to land on fertile soil, an extension of the Jacob's ladder is possible.

The wild roses put even more energy into assuring the survival of their species. In August the juicy, plump and sweet, orange-red rose hips will attract many a wild rose planter. These rose hips are the largest fruit of any native plant around here. One rose bush might offer 30 or 40 fruits, each holding at least four seeds. That's up to 160 chances at making a new rose bush. If only one out of every 100 seeds succeeds, there will be roses enough to carry on.

I've never watched the bluebells close enough to discover how their seeds are carried away. Perhaps they just fall to the ground under the plant. They seem too heavy to be windblown, and I've never noticed anything eating them. I will keep an eye on the bluebells this summer to see what happens.

16

In past years I have investigated other plants. One of the most amazing life cycles is that of the *Splachnum* moss. This unusual moss is easy to identify, and that's saying something when you start looking at mosses. *Splachnum* is about four inches tall, with a red stem and a tiny yellow "China cap" topped off with a red button. My moss book tells me that *Splachnum* grows only on animal manure. The moss emits a "manurial odor" that attracts flies which carry the spores to other droppings.

While *Splachnum* requires a very particular "seed" bed, *Corydalis*, or bleeding heart, follows another path to the perpetuation of its kind. Its seeds are lying around everywhere. The *Corydalis* seed coats are very tough, protecting the contents from rotting in the moist soil. The seeds can lie dormant for 100, even 200 years. When wildfire or some other disturbance alters the land, the seeds grow for it. I have come upon plants that were practically bushes — five feet tall and six feet wide — perhaps reflecting the rich nutrient supply released by the fire. One such plant had been sampled by a moose but found unsatisfactory, as the stems were spit out a few feet away. There may be a chemical inhibitor that discourages wildlife from eating *Corydalis*.

June 11, 54°   Out along the trail I interrupt a spruce grouse family outing. The mother startles me, charging down the hill, carrying on instinctively with all her might to keep my attention. She fans her tail, fluffs out her feathers, whistles, whines, chirps, and scrambles away, dragging her broken wing behind her. Her antics are so dramatic I can hardly take my eyes off her, just as she hopes. I know the brood is probably back where I first saw the hen. I search the vegetation with my eyes and there they are, nearly a dozen obedient chicks, frozen in place, blending in perfectly with the grass and leaves. The hen flaps closer, signaling her young to stay put. Two chicks panic and peep off under a blueberry bush. The other chicks hold their ground, their occasional blinking allowing me to distinguish them from the vegetation. Then, feathers seem suddenly to turn to leaves, and I can see only four chicks where a moment before I counted a dozen.

Mother grouse is frantic, so I follow her farther and farther away from her chicks. Just when I almost catch up to her, the broken wing miraculously gains strength and she bursts ahead another 15 feet, clucking, twitching, and tempting me to follow still farther. "Well done, mama grouse, may you and some of your brood survive the summer. I hope you'll return to the gravel I'll put out for you under the cabin eaves next fall."

June 14, 55°   At the breakfast table this morning, we are startled by an unexpected visitor. Suddenly a chocolate-colored ermine, flashing ebony eyes, inquisitively stares through the screen window, just two feet away from our coffee cups. The firewood pile, stacked level with the window under the eaves, allows the ermine its excellent view. We hadn't seen this weasel since it had lost its winter-white coat. A nosy black nose investigates the smells of our eggs, toast, coffee, and ourselves that float out through the screen. Our spellbound forms do not seem to register as a threat to the ermine. It certainly can see us, but without movement we are just part of the table.

The supple ten-inch body ripples across the birch logs, followed by a four-inch tail, tipped in black. The weasel is entirely alert. It is not alarmed. Small round ears accentuate a wide skull, and a thick neck helps to balance small front quarters and a humped back with the powerful hindquarters. The front legs are short, keeping the body low. We saw that body leaping through the deep snow last winter, leaving spaces of nearly a yard between touchdowns. Those hind legs are well adapted for pouncing on prey. Having decided our eggs and toast are not worthy prey for its breakfast, the ermine dives back down into the dark, secret runways between logs.

Returning to our own now-cold breakfast, we savor the tast of the wild visit, an excellent dash of excitement to flavor the meal.

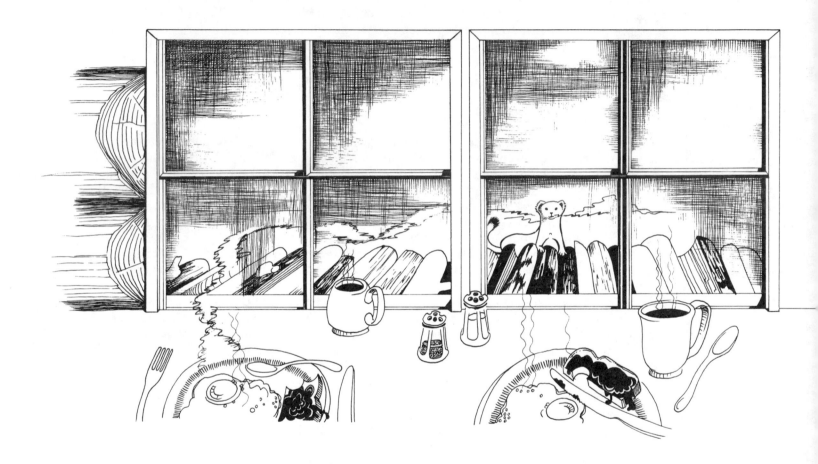

June 16, 62°   Well, that didn't take long! The willows along the creek have produced two- to three-inch leaves, and now I can try my sniffing experiment — "The Nose Knows?" At first sniff the leaves of all species smell alike, so I crumple them in my hand to free the oils and exaggerate the odors. Now I can detect some differences, but when I close my eyes and try again, the distinctions are less certain. Just last week our salad was freshened by some new willow buds. The dark green color enlivened the pale cabbage and carrot salad with its yogurt dressing. My test today is not quite so tasty, and I am

18

satisfied to distinguish only possible differences. I have no doubt the moose can easily tell which willow species is which and I admire this ability. I remember seeing the impressive taste buds along the moose's tongue when we examined his mouth while butchering him last hunting season. It's amazing how each plant and animal is equipped with special talents or adaptations to survive in its own place. However life evolved this far, whether by chance or by direction, the mere reality that it has is answer enough for me.

June 19, 65°   Along the dog trail where I walk this afternoon, a puddle has nearly dried up. A pride, or is it a flock, of tiger-swallowtail butterflies has alighted around the edges of a patch of damp soil. The huge yellow, blue, and black butterflies drink by sucking moisture from this soil, fluttering their wings now and then, perhaps to cool themselves. So quiet and bright and magnificent this afternoon tea party. I regret disturbing them as I pass by. No doubt they will return again shortly after I disappear.

The diamond willow is casting seeds to the wind — thousands, no, millions of them. A half-inch of seed fluff covers the ground. If only one in 1,000 takes root, there will always be an abundance of willows.

The cottonwoods are also floating out millions of seeds, and when the afternoon breeze picks up, the air is a swirl of white seeds, teasing my heart with a summer snowstorm. "Easy does it, Mary. These long sun-days are halfway round the sun from the snow-days of December."

Royal purple flags of wild irises unfurl today, down along the marshy trail. I guess because I first loved irises back in our Wisconsin backyard, they seem too civilized, too domesticated, too regal to be growing as wildflowers here in the swamps. But grow here royally they do, and I am their humble subject, full of admiration.

June 20, 84°   Summer is here! Great white clouds lift up off the hills like a bowl of bread dough forgotten on the warming oven. An afternoon shower would be welcome to cool things off, but no rain falls.

June 21, 73°   *Summer Solstice.* My round calendar is bisected by a straight line connecting today with December 21st, the Winter Solstice. Today can be celebrated for two good reasons: (1) This is the longest day, with the official sunrise at 12:59 a.m. and sunset at 10:48 p.m. (2) Today marks the swing toward winter darkness. Both events deserve recognition.

To celebrate the ultimate energy source for all life on earth, the sun, I hike up above treeline where the sun's path can be followed all night. About 100 miles north of here, nearer the Arctic Circle, the sun will not disappear below the horizon on the Solstice. There at midnight the sun rolls along the edge of the earth but pulls itself up again, continuing the swing into morning and another day. Here on the ridge above our cabin, the sun disappears for a little more than two hours, but the sky stays light with a glowing, quiet enchantment.

Above treeline the alpine tundra is at peak production this third week of June. A horizon-to-horizon carpet of wildflowers rolls out in full bloom. Most plants are less than six inches high, "small, but oh my!" The miniatures must be rugged to survive up here, yet they appear so delicate and humble.

Dryas, or mountain avens as it is commonly called, predominates in this carpet, forming extensive mats of creamy white blossoms, each only three inches high. The gray-green scalloped leaves gather up solar energy and use it to create wind flowers. A few of these flowers have already dropped their petals. During stormy weather or a decrease of light, the numerous long feathery seeds twirl tightly closed, protecting the embryo at the bottom of each. When the weather clears or brightens, the feathers unwind, letting the seeds mature in the dry air. On the night of the Solstice, this twirling will have little rest. I wonder if *Dryas* seeds in the southern hemisphere twirl the other direction because of the Coriolis effect.

Pincushions of moss campion crowd together, trying to break the world's record for how many pink blossoms can dance on the head of a pinnacle of tundra. I go down on my knees and nuzzle my nose deep into some of the cushion contestants, as if an abundance of perfume gives the extra points needed to break the record. Infections of curly louseworts grow in bunches. Rock jasmines grow alone, here and there. In the rocky outcroppings, exotic ferns flourish, as well as the aromatic, deep purple azaleas. Below the rocks, often where a little drainage offers a drink, the perfect, off-white bells of heather dangle down from their squared-off leaves.

Looking in every direction I see new kinds of flowers. This high world of diminutives is a most beautiful example of the sun's handiwork, an excellent spot for a Solstice celebration. To make the event complete, I search for my two favorite tundra flowers. With so many beauties it is difficult to love one more than the other, but the mountain bistort, or pink plume, tickles my fancy. The plume is only about five inches tall, with many small, vividly pink blossoms spiraling around the upper two or three inches. Pink plumes are extravagant but fairly common and easy to find.

My other favorite plant is not common at all. This variety grows on the driest, windiest, highest summits. I must climb to the very top to hope to find this one. It is not flashy. I've only seen it growing in small clumps, perhaps two to three inches in diameter. At the peak of its bloom this alpine wonder radiates a deep blue more luminous than any sky I have ever seen. Perhaps the blue is enhanced by the orange-red center, dashed with a light yellow. The alpine forget-me-not has the truest name of any flower. Once you have climbed up to find a dwarf forget-me-not, you won't. The memory of this night in the sun will warm me on many a cold dark day next winter.

As for the second significance of this day, the beginning of the darkness, I will honor the coming darkness by closing my eyes and falling asleep right here tonight, this night of no night, on this carpet of wildflowers. My face will rest in blossoms. My nose will enjoy the sweet air. On this high, bright moment of summer, I will daydream of a still, dark night waiting on the other side of the year. To appreciate the light, one needs to understand and love also the dark and the earth's round roll from one to the other.

June 28, 80°   An uneasy smell of woodsmoke drifts in from the west. "Uneasy," I say, because this is much more than a swirl of smoke from a stovepipe. This is the smell of wildfire. The sun months, May, June, and July, are the season for wildfires. Lightning from high thunderclouds strikes the ground and ignites the dry fuel waiting there. The clouds are so high their rainfall evaporates before reaching the earth. The temperature cools only a little during the night, what there is of night, and the land remains dry.

By noon today the air is heavy and hazy. The sun flattens into an eerie orange disk. At first, my gut feeling is one of fear, but my mind knows better. Indeed, the radio reports the fire is west of Fairbanks some 200 miles. But smoke so thick this far away means it is a huge one.

Wildfire has been, is now, and probably always will be an important natural force in Interior Alaska. Fire rejuvenates the forest by interrupting the process of *plant succession*, the gradual change in the kinds of plants dominating a location. As I walk through the different forest succession stages in our valley, I can usually find evidence of old fires, like the charred stumps of standing blackened trunks. These different-aged forests offer a variety of homes for wildlife, and the diversity in the whole ecosystem is healthy. Without wildfire, most of Interior Alaska would be covered by a single forest type, old-growth spruce. Many creatures cannot survive in this advanced stage alone. They need the herbs, shrubs, saplings, and deciduous trees of younger stages. Wildfire creates a mosaic of different forest types which in turn promotes a variety of animals.

This smell of fire is the smell of change.

July — Something New Under the Sun

July 3, 70°   The flute-like songs of the Swainson's thrush float out through the light rain this evening. The round, swirly notes seem amplified by the raindrops. Their singing in the rain sounds good. All the other birds are quiet now, their courting and nest building over, and it is good that the thrushes have the air to themselves. It is also good to wake in the night, listen to the thrush lullabies, and then drift back to sleep, dreaming on the round, ethereal melodies, sweet dreams every time. The thrush songs are perfect accompaniments to the low glow of the night sun in July.

July 5, 89°   The canoe rides high in the water with our light load packed in the center. The 60-foot-long gillnet is neatly coiled in an old washtub, our packs and boxes of food wedged in around it. Hopefully, on our return trip, the washtub will hold some king salmon.

   We cast off on the Chena River, a tributary of the Tanana. Being on the water seems the best place to be in this hot weather. John mans the stern while I paddle in the bow. In front of me rides Schniptzel, a 75-pound husky, our honorary guest on this trip. He seems not to understand that he is on vacation, off duty. He insists on being the ever-responsible lead dog, standing at attention, watching eagerly for driftwood floating along in the river. I'm tempted to give him the dog-mushing command "Gee!" to see if he'll leap overboard and swim off to the right.

   After a half-hour's paddling in the hot sun, we need to cool off. We pull into an abandoned raft which is tied to some cottonwoods on shore. John dives into the water, surfacing with a "Whuuueeeeeee!" I slip in more gradually and swim like crazy to warm up. After the first numbing minutes, I am comfortable. Friend Schniptzel remains in the canoe and whimpers. John unties the canoe's rope to let the dog drift along with us in the current. Before we reach the mouth of the Chena, we climb back into the canoe, much to Schniptzel's relief. I want to shake off and get even for all the times he soaked me this way, but I just can't get the hang of it. The hot sun feels good now and our clothes soon dry.

The confluence of the Chena and Tanana rivers is a meeting of two worlds. The juncture looks like a trickle of weak tea pouring into a cauldron of old coffee, thick with cream. The Chena tea is mostly rainwater draining off the hills northeast of Fairbanks. The Tanana coffee travels farther. Its headwaters are brewed high in the Alaska Range, near the Canadian border, with one fork beginning in the Yukon Territory. July's hot weather melts the snow pack in the mountains, and the resulting runoff trickles down through cracks in the glaciers to under-ice channels. These forces of glacier ice and water grind away the mountains and "something's gotta give." The mountains yield, tumbling boulders, rocks, pebbles, gravel, sand, and ultimately silt into the tributaries that converge to make the Tanana. The load of silt remaining in suspension is what makes the river coffee colored.

As our canoe turns out into the Tanana, I can hear those little bits of the mountains bumping along beneath us, scouring the canoe hull. The Tanana coffee boils and churns along, swirling in the Chena tea. In a matter of yards no evidence of the Chena is visible. Yet there must be something — a smell, a texture, a taste — for every year thousands of salmon swimming by this corner turn 90° to the left and swing up into the Chena, to return to the gravel bars and fresh water of their own hatching. How they find their way some 1500 miles upstream from the ocean is a wonder.

The Alaska Department of Fish and Game's "Wildlife Notebook Series" gives good information on the salmon's life cycle. The females excavate nests in the gravel and deposit thousands of eggs, which the males immediately fertilize. By early spring the eggs have hatched and the young fish live in the gravel until they absorb the food in their attached yolk sacs. In early spring these juveniles, called fry, swim up through the gravel and feed on plankton and insects for the following year. In their second spring, the fish head downstream to the ocean. These migrants are called smolt. Once in the ocean, the salmon feed on fish and crustaceans and grow rapidly.

Salmon may be ready to reproduce when as young as two years or as old as seven years. After they have spawned, all king salmon die and move on in the ecosystem, perhaps in a quick bite by a black bear, or in the many smaller bites of smaller fish or other creatures in the spawning streams.

We will try our best to intercept some of the kings before they spawn. John starts the ten-horse motor and we travel downstream to inspect the eddies, or backwaters, we have fished before. Some are silted in by the restless Tanana. The river changes constantly, picking up material in one place and depositing it again downstream. We agree on a good eddy and attach one end of the net to a sturdy alder on shore. Next we move out into the current. We hope to place the net exactly along the outer edge of the eddy, but the current is far stronger than our motor. When the net is stretched tightly, John gives the signal and I heave the heavy rock anchor overboard. Ker-splasssh! The outer ten bobbers disappear but rise again in half a minute. We pull ourselves back to shore along the net, tugging at it to test for tangles. "Looks good," we agree.

We set up camp on shore overlooking the net. Occasionally, a fish splashes in the net and we are hopeful of a good run. Schniptzel barks at the splashing from his spot by the cooking fire. Gulls complain on the island across from camp. A pair of arctic terns chases them off, and quiet returns. Just the constant sound of the river passing by. Summer fish camp on the river feels good, a seasonal tradition people have always enjoyed in Alaska.

We check the net next morning. Our net is really made to catch the smaller chum salmon. The weave expands to six-inch holes, rather than the eight inches of a real king net, and we catch more of the smaller fish. The 30-, 40-, and 50-pounders bounce off our net and escape. But this morning we are lucky, as six 10- to 15-pound fish are waiting, plus a bonus of one giant near 30 pounds. Several fish are already stiff, having drowned during the night. Others put up a good struggle, and we are careful to hang on tightly as we work them out of the net. The kings are magnificent fish, enormous and powerful. Their two- to three-foot bodies are rosy red with black or dark-green flecks. They turn this color as they get close to their spawning grounds. Do they know how close they are? Do they already sense the special waters of the Chena? A quick blow to the head quiets them, although some continue to flop in the boat. John assures me this is just a reflex, but I club them again, determined to end the pain. I feel quite barbaric, killing another living creature with my own bare hands and a piece of driftwood. Still, this is a reality I prefer to a can of tuna. I take these living creatures respectfully and gratefully.

We clean the salmon in the mouth of a clear creek, saving the heads for the sled dogs waiting back home. White-faced wasps are attracted to the flesh, and we work as quickly as possible. The dorsal fin is removed, identifying the fish as caught for subsistence purposes. No doubt the burbot, scavengers of the Tanana, will gather here and clean up the entrails. Life flows on.

We return upstream with our river harvest. I watch the surface of the water for salmon traveling with us. I know there are thousands of fish in that water, yet I see none of them. Good luck, my slippery swimmers. May you slip past the dappled shadows that chase you and find your way home.

Wooden fishwheels along the shore turn and creak, their wire baskets plopping over and over with the current, scooping up fish. There is a timeless feeling on the river and we return filled with an old quiet.

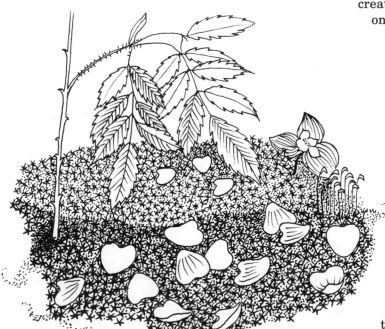

July 8, 74°   A sprinkling of pale pink petals rests on the green moss beneath the wild rose bushes. The colors create a striking combination of ephemeral rose on evergreen moss. I will recall this wonder when I pass by again this winter on snowshoes.

July 9, 82°   "Sneeders," as we affectionately call the many kinds of dragonflies, zoom around, clearing the air of excess insects. They maneuver like tiny helicopters, hovering for an instant in front of my nose, and then veering off on some important mission, their vibrant bodies sparking in the air with iridescent blue and green. Sneeders are certainly the flashiest creatures around.

As a child, I falsely believed that dragonflies could sew my eyes shut (no doubt a warning given me by my older brother). Years later, even though I knew this was impossible, I had to force myself to give up the myth.

Today the sun is steaming off my energy, threatening to boil away my day, so I go down to the thermokarst pond, looking for the coolness of the water. Approaching quietly, in hope of glimpsing the family of green-winged teal, I settle near the shore. No teal today — the place seems vacant — and then, only two feet in front of my eyes, I spy a still, prismatic blue dragonfly, quietly resting on the leaves of a tall sedge. The two-inch slender body is brilliant as the transparent wings fold away. Then my eyes catch a sparkle of more blue, hundreds of resting blue dragonflies spattered on the green leaves. I admire them for several moments, until a quick movement to defend myself from the incessant mosquitoes alarms the sleeping beauties. They swarm off in a blue cloud.

Now that I have seen the gentle blue resting on wet green, I can no longer fear for my eyes. That myth is sewed shut and I can see sneeders for what they really are.

July 13, 84°   The evening demands that we cook outside on an open fire. A cool breeze keeps the bugs down, and the evening concert of songbirds is well worth listening to. As we rest our backs against the picnic tree, a high movement catches both our attentions at the same instant. "What was that?" I ask, and John shakes his head.

"Too small to be a bird. What else could it be? How about a bat?" John responds. We watch the heavens and, sure enough, another tiny creature whirls between the trees at an amazing speed, far too fast to catch in the binoculars. We wait batless another half hour. Later that night I find an old "Wildlife Watcher's Newsletter," from the Nongame Program of the Department of Fish and Game. An article on bats reports five species in Alaska, with the little brown bat most common. Half a million mosquitoes may be consumed in a single night by 500 of these tiny (about one-third ounce) creatures. With this new information, we immediately begin designing a new belfry.

July 14, 74°   Last night the dogs alerted us to the cabbage addict attempting to raid our garden. A young cow moose had stepped over the gate and made her way under the arch, of course the weakest point in our eight-foot-tall fence. John and I came to the rescue of our cole family, threatening the cow with sticks of kindling. We weren't about to go inside the fence with her, so we chased around the outside of the chickenwire and pelted her with more firewood, herding her back over the gate. After a few more mouthfuls, she pivoted around, casually stepped under the arch, and ambled out the trail, stopping here and there to grab a mouthful of willows, as if to say "Relax already, I'm leaving, I'm leaving . . . and thanks for the cabbage."

July 17, 80°   Bugs seem to be thinning out. Seldom need the bug dope. Calypso orchids stand erect, with green and brown striped seedpods. The forest floor around them is so covered with leaf litter it's hard to imagine the seeds could find a place to germinate. I wonder if anything dines on orchid seeds — I'll watch and see.

July 18, 78°   On a trip into Fairbanks, I run into some old friends, the sandhill cranes. I haven't seen them since last spring, when they whirled over in great flocks on their way north to summer nesting areas. I wanted to follow them then, over the hills, over the mountains, out into the watery green tundra. But today I find some cranes that stayed in the Interior, stayed right in Fairbanks only two miles from downtown in the Creamers' Fields. The Department of Fish and Game manages the land as the Fairbanks Migratory Waterfowl Refuge. Good for the birds and for people, this hunk of wild, green country. It was a dairy farm in the early days of Fairbanks and almost got turned into a subdivision in the late '60s. But the residents and the legislature joined efforts and saved the land for the wild things and the people who valued them.

About a dozen birds were working their way across the field today. They strutted along, constantly grazing on the young barley shoots growing in the field and no doubt the insects that thrived beneath this tall green cover. The birds seemed to move with partners, but I never spotted any young. I surmised they were immature birds. The pairs would come and go, perhaps cooling off in a pond to the north. Their returns to the fields were spectacular. The pair would glide down, wings outstretched to nearly six

feet. They announced their arrivals with clear, piercing bugles, often answered by the other cranes on the ground. Was this in recognition or welcome? When the new arrivals were about ten feet above the waving grains, they'd arch back their long necks, fan their tails and wings, and lower their landing gear — those long, dangling legs. That maneuver brought them to a near vertical position, and once they touched down with one foot, their momentum skipped them along for several yards. After a few moments, the new arrivals blended in with the original flock, meandering across the field. Brown cranes gliding down onto a green field, a colorful image.

July 19, 84°   Climbed the moose hunting tree to see what I could from 25 feet in the air. What a lucky reward for my climb: a moose cow and a calf cooling off in a very small pothole, barely large enough for both of them to be wet at the same time. Perhaps this is a "beginner's lesson" and in a few days they will move deeper into the thermokarst pond. The two of them, sharing that shallow pothole — now that's togetherness!

July 20, 92°   The season has matured. The sense of June's urgent rush is fading. The fireweed have exploded, now in ten inches of royal, magenta blossoms, each one a perfect, miniature orchid. The bottom flowers have dropped their petals and replaced them with slender seedpods. Most of the plants stand three to four feet tall, but a few stretch to over six feet. Amazing what standing in the sun can do for you!

July 21, 88°   A few *yellow* willow leaves waving in the morning sun: surprise!

July 25, 80°   The great summer-sky show is about to begin. Already at 7:30 a.m. the temperature is rising. Perhaps we'll top yesterday's 90°. The sky is a flawless blue bowl inverted over the 100-mile-wide valley of the Tanana River. The sky waits in innocent, pure blue, nearly vibrating with anticipation of the battles to come.

To the south the magnificent snowy mountains of the Alaska Range line up from east to west, facing their opponents, the green, rolling hills of the Tanana-Yukon Uplands just north of Fairbanks. Both sides have won my respect. Sometimes I take sides, even cheering one on to victory. An afternoon cloudburst is a refreshing break from the heat.

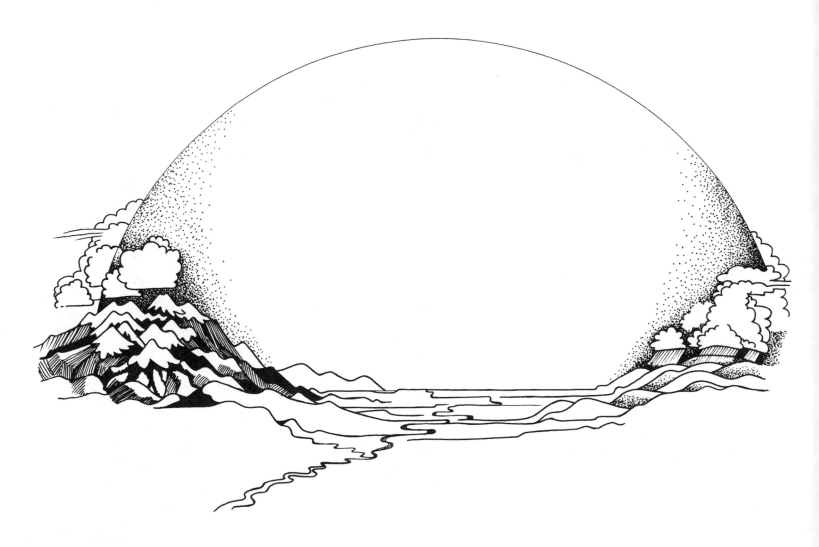

By ten o'clock tufts of white cumulus are breaking over the two high fortresses, scouting out the battlefield. As the sun heats up the air through the morning, the clouds gather courage and momentum. Up and out, billow and bulge, the white forces mass up and over, soaring higher and higher, like genies called out by the power of some unknown commander. The robust white clouds against the deep blue sky look rich and full.

Today the northern force wins quickly and by two o'clock a steady downpour cools the earth. The tensions of the heated morning are released in the rain. By 3:30 the sky brightens, and by late tonight the sky may be clear again. Invigorating, this variety of weather, and intriguing to this cloud watcher.

July 27, 65°   Berries forming on highbush cranberry and blueberry. Most of the berries are still green, with the exception of the red currants. They are ready to pick and easy to pick as they hang in clusters of five to ten berries. The currant patches are pungent with strong, musky currant scent. I easily collect a dishpan-full in two hours. Currants add up quickly for two reasons: (1) you can grab whole handfuls at a time, and (2) currants don't taste very good raw. Now with blueberries and raspberries, it is easy to eat a few, save a few, eat a few more. . .

July 29, 65°   Families of sparrows and juncos flit and hop around under the trees. The fledglings are nearly the size of their parents, yet their scruffy plumage and slightly awkward movements attract my attention. Feeble "I am a white crown sparrow" calls come now and again, but usually the pattern is weak or even missing some of its notes. The pleading has mellowed from early summer singing, when in May and June the whole future of sparrow-dom depended on that singing.

I hear cranes calling with that sense of encouragement the cooler weather brings on. July is slipping by and the earth is rolling away from the high sun of the Solstice. My eyes are looking for more yellow leaves. Oh, I enjoyed the bright green world, the sweet flowers, the families of creatures, the long days with never-ending daylight, when a day seemed longer than just 24 hours. But I confess I am eager for autumn, anxious to roll the Wall Journal over another 30° to the left. I am ready for a change.

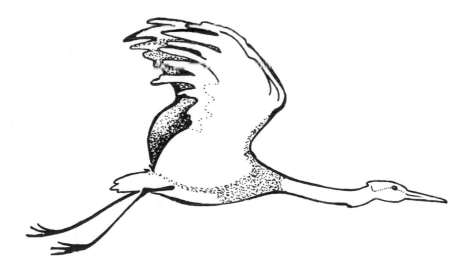

August — A Gust of Change

<u>*Aug. 2, 70°*</u>   *August* — the word has a nice ring to it, a welcome crispness after the sumptuous splurge of summer's *June* and *July*. The time has come to rotate my round calendar, putting August on the top. Time will come full circle and the seasons will encircle time.

August sounds like an arctic gust roaring down from the north, nipping the willow leaves yellow and shivering their stems to maroon — a nice combination for the season. We'll see what the month holds, what August unfolds.

<u>*Aug. 5, 58°*</u>   Now I am enjoying the long, yellow days of summer. The season had been generous with its wonders. But this morning a fresh smile shapes my expression, surprises me, reminds me of last night.

On my last trip out before bed, I was listening to the quiet in the woods. The birds were busy now, no singing, no courting. The air was almost chilly, not a real nip, but a certain slight shiver. The thermometer admitted only 48°. The night sky was a soft relief to my eyes, not a definite darkness, but an honest dusk. Then my eyes caught a faint sparkle of a star — then another, and still one more. "Star light, star bright, first star I see tonight. . . "The incantation came automatically, still on the tip of my tongue after two and a half months without stars. So did my wish.

Now this morning, with an irresistible smile puckering my cheeks and the inside confidence of the stars, I wonder if my wish will be granted? Will the winter's snows come deep and early?

<u>*Aug. 8, 50°*</u>   The fireweed-works begin the third act of their show. The seedpods ripen from the bottom of the stalk up, following the same pattern as did the blossoms. A few purple petals still wave from the

30

top of an occasional plant. True, those flamboyant flowers celebrated the summer well, but the perfect symmetry of the plump seedpods expresses the maturity of August more appropriately. The lowest pods, each about three inches long, have split open along parallel seams. The slender strips of pod curl back, presenting to the sunny world hundreds of ultralight seeds lined up and waiting.

Once the pods have split open, the seemingly impatient seeds are eager to ride the wind. Those at the outer end cast off first, trusting their downy rotors to carry them off to a future on some speck of open soil. This is the very stage that draws me closer; the balanced anticipation of those fireweed dreams waiting for their turn to connect the past with the future. I blow a gentle puff and the white parachutes open and carry away a hundred more of the precious cargo. I applaud this grand finale of the flowers. This population explosion tickles my fancy, and my nose.

Aug. 10, 37°   This morning I track the advance guard of autumn, those hungry nocturnal scouts sent out in the guise of frost. The cool air slips down the hills and swirls along our footpath. As long as the air keeps moving it stays warm, but here and there it settles in the dips and valleys of the trail to rest a while, nibbling on the vegetation where it naps, nibbling with a frost-bite.

Now where a moose rests there remains a swirly, cozy nest of pressed grass, ringed by some ragged willows chewed off as an evening snack. Where the frost scouts rest, the morning finds limp, dark horsetails surrendering to the weight of the winter guard. Horsetails, the first plants to rise up out of the brown earth in April, are also the first to lie down as part of the blanket covering the hardening earth.

My feet feel where the frost has slept and my eyes follow the edge of dark horsetails. Under the earth these plants are alive and well; only this year's growth has succumbed. Hopefully many of them have produced spores that invaded new patches of soil. Horsetails get their work done early, with no fear of frost.

In the garden the squash plants are also nipped around the fringy edges of their huge leaves, but there are still plenty of green cells working. Nevertheless, the garden has been warned.

Aug. 11, 44°   More yellow leaves popping out on the willows. The last raspberries fall to the ground. Happy shrews!

Aug. 13, 54°   The August monsoons have set in: four gray, rainy days in a row. The ground is squishy under foot. At last a good time to catch up on indoor chores. I feel cozy sitting at the kitchen table which, in a one-room cabin isn't necessarily a *kitchen* table, but I think of it that way. A fire crackles in the cookstove and the heat feels good. Bread rises in the warming ovens above the stove.

Now evening, it is dark enough to need the kerosene lamps for the first time this summer. Their yellow glow brightens as the outside light fades, confirming another sun passage.

31

Aug. 17, 52°   Always an exception, always a free spirit in nature — amid the brown grass one more dandelion stands up for sunshine.

Aug. 19, 63°   On my round calendar, April and August share two special events: stars and geese. On the 5th I saw my first stars and today my whole spirit thrills to the sight of wild geese. I am working in the carrot patch, thinning out the stragglers for dinner. I hear the geese before I see them, and the closer they come the more determined their urging calls sound. They are certain of their journey. Frosty nights on the nesting grounds to the north have given the signal. Perhaps those first twinkling stars have also beckoned them.

I watch the geese waver over my garden, each bird beating its wings steadily. How can they keep that up for 3-4,000 miles? The flock dissolves into two unbalanced V's and then magically weaves itself back together again. I can almost hear their wings pushing the air, almost feel the blast on my face. I squint after them as they vanish into the southeast. The day changes, the season swirls. My spirit is swept up; I fly a little today.

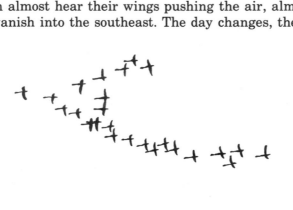

Aug. 21, 63°   I have been expecting the wave of yellow warblers to flow through my garden any day, as they have in Augusts past, and today they came. I have only noticed them the past four years, but no doubt they have been passing through this way long before this garden was planted.

This morning a flurry of small wings brings in a band of 15-20 warblers. I can only identify three kinds, but of course there are more. The yellow-rumped, the Townsend's, and the canary king himself, the yellow warbler, these I see for sure. The females are a greener shade of yellow and they disappear, well camouflaged in the leaves. The tiny birds dart between the graceful dill plants, land on the fence rail for a short rest, and then zoom up to the tall sunflowers, which just stand there nodding over the cabbage patch. The warblers seem nervous, and somehow they tend to stay near the leaves and flowers of their own hue. They chirp incessantly, flitting their tails as they feed. But this is no daily feeding excursion. I suspect these warblers have begun their long journey south, and some of their anticipation stays in the air of this garden after the yellow birds have flapped away.

Last year, at the same moment the warblers came, a chocolate-brown snowshoe hare also visited. It thumped down the path (alas, it still had on its snowshoes) in a zigzagging approach. The hare disappeared under the squash plants for a few minutes and then ventured over to the flowers. (Luckily the other vegetables were protected by a fence.) The hare snuggled down the rows between the flowers, nose wiggling, whiskers feeling for petals. Passing up the pansies, the hare tasted a marigold but spit out the golden tidbits. At last it found the purple violas, exactly what it was looking for. The hare systematically set about clipping off each stem at the base and then nibbled out to the blossom, devouring each purple petal in turn. Fascinated, I watched my flowers disappear one by one. As the warblers had preferred yellow, this hare was partial to purple. Such particular fancies are realized in this patch of garden!

Aug. 24, 52°   Most of the native plants are going to seed now. They have matured into their subtle colors of tan and brown. "Most of the plants," I say, because there is one definite exception: the blue gentian. This simple five-petaled star-shaped flower is just beginning to bloom. It grows in disturbed areas, along the dog trail or old abandoned roads, right in among the grasses. A humble setting for such a remarkably beautiful flower. Walking along through the dry grasses, I am always surprised to find the pale blue beauties nodding their blossoms among the "weeds." I think it must be the honest shade of blue that I admire so much and the contrast of the pale blue and the dark stem. At night the blossoms close up tightly, a behavior not needed in June and July by the summer flowers. But this is not the late bloomer of summer; this is the first and only bloomer of autumn.

Aug. 27, 48°   A hard frost will come tonight, the radio warns. We harvest the squash, dill, lettuce, and less hardy flowers. Those brave bright marigolds, my favorites, which seemed immortal yesterday, wait helpless today. I will cover them with dogfood bags, but they will suffer even so. The clear night provides incentive to act.

Aug. 28, 50°   Highbush cranberry leaves vary in shades of scarlet to maroon, and their fragrance saturates the air. The musty, pungent, non-compromising smell finalizes the season. Clusters of ten to 20 brilliant berries dangle from two-inch stems.

Yellow bouquets of birch leaves pop out along the green branches, ever so slowly wheeling the world toward winter. I have run out of space on my Wall Journal and am eager to roll over to September.

Aug. 29, 30°   A layer of ice seals the yellow birch leaves on top of the water barrel. I tap with my water dipper. Tap, tap again. A gust of arctic air swirls in from the north. August is over.

September — Round the Earth

Sept. 1, 44°   I unpin my calendar and turn September to the top. I like the roundness of it all, the reminder of earth turning round sun, the effects of this huge arc on our small horizon.

Sept. 4, 54°   The puffs of yellow that popped out in the birches last week have radiated out along the branches. Some whole trees have eased into greenish yellow and a few are now more yellow than green. Here and there an aspen flashes a limb of amber or crimson, leaves trembling in the wind and vibrating in color. Last May when these leaves exploded open in tender green, the energy of that explosion held the entire day in the eagerness of sunrise. Today the little explosions bursting out here and there and over there are golden puffs of anticipation of the sunset.

I return to my listening spot under the old aspen on the ridge overlooking the creek. Here is an excellent view of the long valley. Within the first half hour my ears hear the calling and my eyes strain to coordinate. Then, higher than I was looking, the long, powerful chevron of swans streams down the valley, wings wide and steady. Certainly I should be able to spot the young of the year! At only four months old they must be smaller, weaker, slower? And here they are, trying to fly 4,000 miles — impossible. All good sense says it's impossible, yet year after year they do it. The wild cries must urge them on, explaining the mystery of migration and the anticipation of the long shadows that are coming. Though I don't understand their language, their message echoes clearly down the valley long after the swans disappear from sight.

Sept. 7, 40°   Before passing into winter my spirit longs to walk the tundra, above treeline. The variety of color in this autumnal quilt completes the golden harvest, a strikingly different tone from that of

April. Patches of maroon speak up for the blueberry shrubs, red-orange sings out for the dwarf birch, scarlet and crimson scream for the tiny bearberry plants, and the mellow-yellows carry the tune for the willows. Deep golden cottonwoods chime in along the creeks and, of course, the rich bass of the deep-green spruce gives contrast, consistency, and depth to the song of colors. A steady rain intensifies the colors, magnifies the music. A charcoal sky emphasizes contrast well. The tundra celebrates the successful growing season, the production of new seeds to secure the future for each species. The air rings with pure joy of life. This is it!

Sept. 8, 30°   My berrypicking instincts lead me to thick patches. The deep cranberry red acknowledges the frost and my stiffening fingers agree. I pick with one bare hand, alternating the dry mitten. Here and there I see the remains of a vole's berry patch where just the bits of berry skin are left. What gourmets they are. Those clever little fellows have a good way to move cranberries: they just roll them along with their noses. No cold fingers for those harvesters. What would it be like to live under the roots and leaves with the voles? To scurry after your nose, rolling cranberries down into your tunnels, always listening for the dive of a hawk overhead or the pounce of a marten on top of your escape tunnel. To blink at the brightness above and welcome the damp darkness below, knowing each cavern by the feel of your whiskers — this would be a fine life.

Sept. 9, 42°   The forest colors are at their peak. I walk through the familiar woods and, although familiar, some new golden enchantment is overwhelming. Stopping under a tall birch tree, I rest on my back, feeling the roots below me ripple in response to the wind in the high branches. The delicate lacework of yellow leaves against deep-blue sky is entrancing. I soak up the yellows above me as the roots beneath me absorb minerals. Memories of these bright ambers will nourish me someday in the cool blue-white of winter.

   The golden mood is quiet, content, timeless. I let the forest have its way with me.

Sept. 10, 37°   The 4th act of the fireweed-works is complete. Deep maroon leaves have flashed up the stems. Here and there, some leaves are streaked with green.

   Most of the seedpods are empty now and the remaining hulls are curling with age.

   Birch cones droop heavily from the highest branches. Some spruce trees are loaded with cones and the red squirrels are ever busy clipping down their winter's food supply. In the early morning the continual plops of cones hitting the ground map the squirrel's movement. Later in the day the cones will be scurried back to the main middens, those huge mounds of cones formed layer upon layer, year after year. Each midden is honeycombed with extensive tunnels, warm, cozy rest areas to be used when the temperature drops below -30°. The ripe cones are neatly tucked into these tunnels, or under curls of birch bark or any other safe cupboard. The squirrels make me nervous with all their chattering and chasing back and forth. Each animal defends its own territory, and males and females are only tolerant of each other during the breeding season. I admire their energy and resourcefulness, and they are very pretty to look at, bushy tails curled up over their backs. But there is some part of me that resents their constant bickering.

I prefer the squirrels' nocturnal cousins, the flying squirrels. These wide-eyed creatures glide down from the taller spruce at twilight and smack into the trunk of the birdfeeder tree. Then they scamper up the bark with their claws a-clicking. Flying squirrels are not territorial like their cousins. Some nights I have heard two flying squirrels near the bird feeder. Perhaps the pair shares a nest dug out of a witch's broom, a thick, abnormal outgrowth of spruce branches. I wonder if they have a cache of truffles stored in some hollow tree? The flying squirrels dig up these underground fungi during the summer. The shrill flying squirrel call expresses the mystery of the night, of creatures that can see me, when I can't see them.

Sept. 11, 38°   For the past three and a half months this forest has done the impossible: it has made something out of nothing. The unique miracle of photosynthesis unfolds leaf by leaf. The green plants take sunlight, water, and carbon dioxide and transform them into carbohydrates and more leaves, stems, branches, trunks, and roots. You and I can't do this no matter how hard we try. The birch trees can. All we can do is admire the miracle and breathe in the good oxygen given off in the process.

Sept. 12, 44°   We return to a distant creek in the canoe to hunt for our winter's meat supply. Again I repeat my annual questions: How can anything as big as a moose subsist on mere water and plants? This is such a short, simple food chain. And how can anything as big as a moose disappear so easily, simply blend into the willows out of which it appeared?

As we slowly move up the creek, little schools of birch leaves swirl downstream in the main channel, like salmon returning to the sea. We pull in beneath a tall spruce along the shore. John or I climb as high as we dare and look out over the muskeg. The sun is warmer up there, above the shade of the other trees. Looking directly down flutters my stomach — "What am I doing way up here?" I ask. Better to concentrate on more distant views! My heart beats faster from the climb up, and my grip is tighter than necessary.

This bird's-eye view is refreshing. Just once I would like to spring off this tree and glide out over the swamps to land in a distant snag, folding my wings neatly as I plan my next flight. So in my mind I fly, while my body stays hugging the trunk of this tree. A light breeze teases me, stealing some of the precious warmth and tightening my grip on the branches. When one is sitting in a tree, the sound is not the wind through the trees but the wind through the needles.

Camp robbers, relatives of our family back at the cabin, cruise in to investigate me. They land at a safe distance above me in the branches, coo a little as if to say, "My, my, what do we have here?", and then sail off to tell the world.

I try to reason with them, explain that "I'm a friend in good standing with your cousins back in the woods; you can trust me. If only you would share a little information with me, just fly out and land above a lazy bull moose and whistle back to me. That's all I ask. In exchange we'll leave a cache of meat and guts, enough to last you for weeks." But no, they will have nothing to do with my plan. They will not be bribed and act like I'm talking a completely different language. I admire their faithfulness to their neighbors.

By dusk my eyes are failing me, but my ears are eagerly compensating. The creek below, ever constant in the daylight, now sends cryptic messages. "Is that a moose crossing, splashing in the current?" my ears ask. A beaver smacks its tail on the surface of the water, warning its partner of potential danger.

A hawk owl glides by at eye level and for an instant we are looking at each other on common ground, or in common air, to be exact. In that instant my presence is recognized as a danger, and the owl swerves sharply away, out across the muskeg. I stay in my tree, blinking and wide eyed, feeling a bit owly even after this rejection.

"Who-who-who . . . who . . . who," I hoot to John who watches from another tree. This soft signal tells him I am going down to start dinner. Why do we hoot? Would the creatures understand if I just shouted, "Oh, John, I'm going down to start dinner!"? Probably not, and I don't expect we're fooling anybody, but somehow it feels more appropriate.

I build the fire carefully, starting with little shreds of birch bark and spruce twigs from the low, dry branches. Then larger branches are added, and finally big pieces of driftwood washed ashore last spring with the high water of breakup. The ritual unites me with my camps of years gone by. The sweet smell of the woodsmoke, each species giving its own essence, welcomes me home again, home to the green moss bed, the sturdy trunk to lean against for a chair, and the ever-fascinating fire to intrigue my mind. Living with the land comes back easily, surprises me with honest, wholesome feelings.

Sept. 17, 29°   We have looked and listened, hoped and prayed, for four whole days now. But after all we are *hunting*, so we should be willing to hunt: "to pursue, to make a search, to travel over or through in search of prey," as Mr. Webster says. Now, on the morning of day 5, John is climbing the tree in camp while I wait below to start the breakfast fire. I won't risk the smoke warning a nearby moose, so I'll wait until John sends word. The low temperature is testing us, and John looks clumsy weaving his way up through the spruce branches with his big parka catching in the limbs.

I hear John, after a few seconds at the top, scuffling back down, knocking bits of bark and spruce twigs as he comes. Is he just too cold this morning or has he seen something? I can tell by his movements before he hits ground.

"Yes, a bull, only 1,000 yards out, lying down in the willows. I'll stalk him on the ground; you watch him from up in the trees and signal me if he starts to move." John takes off through the willows, rifle in hand, and I start up the tree. I'm shaky and slow but I continue to the top without resting. The light is still poor, but I can make out John below me. The moose is nowhere to be seen. Did our noise tip him off? I can't actually see John's face, but somehow I can follow the little white bow on the front of his hat. He must be watching me often for directions. I shake my head and then suddenly I see the moose, only 400 yards from John, but it is a cow moose!

"Oh, John, don't shoot, it's not the bull," I motion frantically, but he just keeps watching me and moving in the cow's direction. Vooooom, voooom!! Two shots shatter the gray dusk. The cow turns, hesitates for a second, and then trots off away from John, head held high, nose testing the air. Her chestnut calf closes in behind her and they both disappear. Where had they even come from, these walking willows?

John appears in a clearing, walks in the opposite direction of the cow. I see the little white bow still looking up at me. John doesn't even seem to be concealing himself. Has he given up? Was there really a bull there or not? I hoot. John hoots back and waves for me to come.

Navigating through the 12-foot-high willows by echo-location, I finally find my hunter. He is rolling over a small bull moose, spreading it out to begin to clean the gut cavity. I am happily flabbergasted.

"Where did he come from? Did you see me waving you away from the cow?"

"Well no, not exactly. I actually never looked up at the tree. I just kept going toward that tamarack there; I knew he was close by. What cow are you talking about?"

"The cow and calf that ran off to the east! But I kept seeing the white bow on your hat — I couldn't really see your face but I knew you were looking for signals."

"Not exactly. You see, I had my hat on backwards so the brim wouldn't get in my way if I had the chance to sight in on the bull. But let's not worry about that now. We've got a lot of work to do with this fellow."

We carefully remove the guts, especially easing out the huge, explosive stomach. A puncture to that bag of fermented willows would taint the whole butchering job. We both admire the perfectness of the moose, both on the inside and the outside. The long hairy ears, the velvety nose, gigantic nostrils, and the beautiful hide, grading from dark brown, almost black on the legs to a warmer brown on the back. One leg has a few porcupine quills protruding around the hoof, hinting at a recent encounter. We guess by his general size and the size of his antlers that the bull is two years old. Plenty for the two of us to pack back to the canoe. We quarter him and divide the rest into manageable portions. The long, slender legs, with their neat hoofs and two sharp toenails are so perfect. So gentle was this creature of the willows. I feel partly sad for taking his life, while I also feel connected to the food chain of this country. I am an omnivore; I need both meat and plants. I want that pot of moose stew simmering on the woodstove this winter. I'd rather get my meat this way and be fully responsible for the killing, even though I'm faced with the blood on my hands.

Wildlife biologists have learned that more than half of the moose born each spring will die before the end of the year. The biologists count the moose from airplanes and have seen this to be true year after year. Lack of good habitat explains some of the loss. Natural predators take some moose. Cold, deep snow winters take others. Old age, accidents, disease, and parasites claim still more. And people, hunters who eat moose meat, we also take some. What a privilege to be part of and to enjoy this food chain, to be related to the willows and the sunlight through this moose meat. I take this from the land and with the energy it gives me, I try to respect and give back to the land in my own ways. With this privilege, I take this responsibility. Fair is fair.

Sept. 18, 30°   A serious breeze from the Alaska Range blasts in this morning, shivering the leaves down from the trees. We load the canoe and head home. Good to be moving out before the weather takes a turn for the worse. Even with all of our warm clothing on, we are cold. The canoe responds sluggishly with the extra passenger, 500+ pounds (a quarter of a ton) of moose, but we are grateful to be heavy.

By lunch the wind has let up and we relax a little in the sun's faint warmth. The leaves continue to patter down, tumbling against the branches and then lightly smacking the ground. The main channel of the creek is a steady swirl of yellow now. Deep eddies along the bank are completely covered over with leaves. In the past five days the whole character of the creek has changed. Nearly all of the leaves are down, but rather than mourn their passing I delight in what they reveal: the marvelous silhouettes of birch trees. The delicate, intricate frameworks, gracefully bowing, bending, arching, drooping, please my gaze and confirm the everlasting strength of trees. Yes, the leaves were beautiful in their bounty, splendid in their radiance, but the simplicity and integrity of these bare branches against the gray sky are quietly overwhelming.

And just as I think I know all the beauty the birch can give, my eye catches the hearts. At the tip of each branch one leaf remains, gently waving in the breeze. Each leaf dangles like a golden heart. How have I missed this in all the autumns past?

We paddle all day, quietly witnessing the peak of the leaf-drop days. It is good to be part of this change, to feel the earth rolling over toward winter.

Sept. 23, 30°   Home. *Fall Equinox.* The light has returned to the forest. I walk my familiar trails, marveling at the changes that occurred while we were hunting. Most of the leaves have fallen and now form the forest carpet. Sunlight streams through the high branches, flooding the golden ground. Today is the Fall Equinox, a point to balance the turning point of March. The sun is at the same place in the sky as in March, but the feel of the forest is completely different. Now there is a quiet satisfaction, a contentment, a relaxation after a busy, productive summer. In just four months these plants have reproduced for another generation; thousands upon thousands of seeds have been created, and the forest will continue. The trees themselves seem to offer a new presence, a strong, patient, timeless presence. I feel welcome among them and I am overwhelmed by the simple peace of the place.

Sept. 25, 25°   In a natural clearing in the forest a tangle of wild roses celebrates their place in the sun. Almost all the leaves have fallen and the prickly maroon stems remain entangled, discouraging all intruders. Amid this threatening, uninviting thicket, one defiant fuchsia blossom hangs on, truly the last rose of autumn. I wonder at it.

September 26, 28°   The deep maroon blueberry leaves are etched with frost this morning. The trail is hard under foot; puddles hold ice. Snow flurries come and go at will all morning. A few juncos still hop about. How will they ever make it south now in freeze-up? Black-bear droppings on the trail are loaded with scarlet highbush cranberries. I'll have to keep my eyes open when I go berrypicking. Good way to spread highbush cranberry plants, I must admit. While we were moose hunting, a bear has rubbed on the log ends of the shop — slightly wavy brown hairs remain on the rough wood. Probably a brown-phase black bear, although it might have been a grizzly.

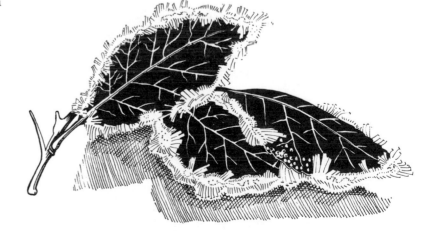

Grouse spring up from the creek bed where they're after the gravel in the shallow water. These tiny pebbles work as a food processor in the grouse's gizzard. Over the lifetime of the bird, the pebbles are worn down and the sharp edges are smoothed off. Each time we eat a grouse, we inspect the gizzard to speculate on the age of the bird by comparing the erosion of the pebbles. Such fine, pretty little specks of quartz. They do seem to select bits of quartz over other rock types. Perhaps I should be more selective when I haul up the packfuls of creek grit that I put under the cabin eaves for the grouse. This autumn ritual assures many grouse visits throughout the coming winter.

Sept. 28, 30°   The fireweed-works are in their last act. The long leaves pale to a dull red color and curl up to match their seedpods. Thanks for the fireworks.

Sept. 30, 35°   The golden days are over, and now my eyes are eased by the earth tones of the land: white, gray, brown, maroon, green, and black. The blending of these subtle colors sets a soothing mood. The individual colors challenge me to look more closely in order to separate them. Dead trunks of alder host bright-yellow, green, and gray lichens, whose colors are intensified by last night's drizzle. These humble, down-to-earth colors have always been there, but the glory of the leaves concealed them, overshadowed them. _Or_ I didn't know how to look for them, nor for the birds' nests that now appear everywhere. Imagine, for half the summer these round nurseries have been crowded with four or five hungry, squawking nestlings, and I never saw them. By mid-July the fledglings had outgrown their togetherness and by mid-August most of them were ready to depart for winter homes to the south. By now some of them are halfway round the earth.

Round the earth. Autumn has set in the west with an evening sundown. Winter is waiting in tomorrow's sun-up. Round the earth.

October — The Waiting Is Over

Oct. 2, 25°   7:30 a.m. The cabin is dark except for the pools of light pouring from the two kerosene lamps onto the table where I work. I get up, cross the cabin to the cookstove for a cup of coffee, and as I turn, my eye catches an ever-so-faint glow in the southeastern sky. The promise of the sunrise holds my attention. I take my hot coffee and a warm parka out onto the woodpile and wait for the sky to wake up.

Second by second the horizon changes. Dark silhouettes of spruce trees stand up before the maize-blue stripe of light. The curve of the horizon against this back lighting reminds me of the roll of the earth into winter.

The light expands until soon there is more yellow than dark. The yellow eases into pale pastels: pink, salmon, and light blue. I watch the greatest show on earth from the best seat in the house, or out of the house as this happens to be. The colors intensify, detailing the delicate patterns of branch and bough in the foreground. These are the long, slow colors of a winter sunrise, one of the most precious attributes of the low sun and shorter days.

Oct. 5, 33°   Today I am comforted again by the soothing, down-to-earth colors of the bare hills, the browns, tans, grays, maroons, and dark greens. Dark leaves are rimmed with frost. I want to dress in forest green and walk among the trees, to blend in and join the honest colors in their subtle simplicity. The earth is waiting, waiting for winter.

Oct. 8, 39°   Any day. Any day very soon these low gray clouds will soften and fall apart. Then the rain will fall from the warm, high air, down through the cooler air, the cold air, and the freezing air. At last the wonder of all those perfect white crystals balancing over and under each other . . . at last the wonder of snow will be here. Everything is waiting.

In the forest thousands of red-backed voles and dusky shrews wiggle and scurry under the frosty brown leaves. These tiny mouse-like creatures are dependent on the safety and insulation of the snow cover to come. Once the great white blanket is spread, these small tunnelers will be quite comfortable. Warmed by the earth's rising heat and trapped by the snow blanket, the air in their runways remains suitable, with temperatures never much below freezing.

Snowshoe hares are also waiting. Their long, flat ears already twitch in new white fur, and their hopping-folding legs silently thump along their secret paths in a matching color. The rest of their bodies still show blotched remnants of summer brown.

Coveys of ptarmigan flush at the sound of my crunching footsteps in the frozen moss. Their once invisible summer plumage is also beginning to molt to the safety of white, quite obvious against the brown willows. I wonder if they are uneasy as they wait for better coordination with the season.

Moose are still in the rut. I think I can smell where the great bulls have passed, thrashing their broad antlers on the shrubs. In the cold morning air I have heard them grunt and snort, challenging all suitors and courting the gentle brown cows.

This morning I found a round bed, seven feet across, swirled down in the tall grass on the edge of the creek. The branches of the feltleaf willow that grows there were nipped short, telling me that this bed probably did not belong to a bull, for they seldom eat during the rut. The matted grass in that bed was smooth and not wet or frosty like the surrounding grass. The nest looked inviting. I wanted to try it out, take a little snooze in a moose bed, visions of Goldilocks dancing in my head. Had I just awakened the sleeping beauty? Was she waiting in the willows close by? Waiting for the winter I anxiously longed for, or waiting for me to move on down the valley so she could return to her warm, dry bed?

The sharp-eyed weasel rippling in and out of our woodpile has put on its rich ermine furs for winter. The sparkly eyes and black-tipped tail are the only contrast.

Oct. 10, 34°   A fine dusting of snow this morning. My friend Jim Anderson calls this "sneaves," the mixture of snow and leaves on the ground. By 9:30 a.m. the snow has disappeared.

Oct. 12, 38°   Today I cut dry, golden grass down by the creek where it grows in tall, thick bunches, some places reaching over my head. The hay will assure sweet dreams for the sled dogs this winter. They love to tromple down their fresh nests in their doghouses. They hardly wait til I am done putting the hay inside. Round and round they circle, until the hay is just right.

My quiet rhythm of slicing the hay with the old sickle, a family heirloom brought from the farm back in Wisconsin, is conducive to daydreaming. The old tool, weathered and used, still serves me well, and I feel close to others who have cut with this sickle or any sickle. I bundle the hay with twine and hang it in the alders to await a ride back to the cabin in a dogsled. Back at my cutting, my thoughts are severed by an urgent bleating from the dark sky above. A determined chevron of geese pushes down the wind toward the southeast. I can hear their wings fanning the air, each bird following in the slipstream of its windbreaker. They urge each other on with desperate cries, as if they understand how late they are, how close behind them winter looms. Have they awakened to new snow in the Yukon Valley this morning?

Today is my 40th birthday, and for the most part I am at peace with the patient world around me, waiting for winter. Yet a part of me takes wing with these wild geese, wary of the coming cold.

Oct. 14, 28°   THE WAITING IS OVER! The gray clouds have opened up and winter has tumbled down during the night. This morning I woke up to blink out at two inches of bright, fresh, silent snow. The supreme season of the North has returned.

As a respectful subject, I venture out to admire the frosty reign. Large crystals balance on every twig, and branches bend low. Instinctively I pull up my parka hood to protect the back of my neck from a surprise shower. Everywhere I look, I am delighted with patterns of life emerging from the snow. Looking up, the delicate lacework of bare, black birch branches is contrasted against the white snow-load. Over the years, each new birch bud stretched out to gain a little more sunlight. The buds grew to twigs, twigs to branches, branches to limbs. Over 100 years of sun-stretching has created this tree, a living, slow-motion ballet lasting far longer than the short dance of my life. With the next puffs of arctic air from the north, the branches will sway and swish free. Gregarious flocks of redpolls will settle there in the branches to sing out the birch seeds. Thousands of these tan fleurs-de-lis will flutter down, leaving a scatter-painting of brown on the snow, tracks of wind, birds, and trees dancing together.

Below the birch, winding through the dense thicket of alders and willows, a snowshoe hare path is already packed down. Several thick-footed nocturnal nibblers have thumped along, leaving their quiet impressions and a few "bunny buttons" — reprocessed willows. I wonder if the hares have completed their molt to white in these last few days. Are they wearing the right coat this morning? I'm not, so I retreat to the cabin, studying my own tracks as I go. What do my wild neighbors think when they cross my tracks? What winter patterns do my own feet follow?

As I come up the hill to the cabin, a swirl of woodsmoke, winter smoke, tickles my nose and swings my eyes up from the snow. The cabin looks cozy with its new sod roof and moss-and-pole chinking between the logs. In the woodshed the dry, quartered birch logs wait on one side and the spruce rounds wait on the other. The birch will be for the heating stove, when it's 10° below zero or colder and we keep a fire going all night. The faster burning spruce will be for the cookstove. Cooking three hot meals a day keeps the cabin warm in most weather.

The high cache holds the dry goods for the next year: rice, noodles, beans, powdered milk, wheat, raisins, seeds, salt, etc. Salmon strips hang in the smokehouse, glazed to a bright, translucent rust color by the alder smoke from two weeks of cool fires. The garden harvest waits in the root cellar, a small,

four- by five-foot room under the center of the cabin. To descend through the trapdoor to fetch vegetables is like going back into summer. The colors and smells of that season have settled in this root cellar.

My winter tracks will travel between these few buildings. They will also turn down to the creek, to chop open the water hole. I am always amazed and grateful for this spring flowing and overflowing over the ice, even at 50° below zero. My tracks will rest coming back up the hill, alongside the round imprints of the heavy water buckets. The water is "supercooled" and the swishing around in the pail, as I carry it back, begins the freezing process. Little plates of ice tinkle together as the small tides subside.

The new snow has softened the trail underfoot and recorded my comings and goings. There are no secrets any more.

Yesterday the earth was hard. Noises bounced back too loudly. Today the snow muffles the noise, softens the sounds. I hear a new quiet in this woods. After sundown the trail will be brighter, the snow reflecting the starlight.

Snow is fair to all, falls evenly on all. Nobody can make the snow come or make it go away. Some people welcome the snow, others curse it, yet snow knows no favorites. Few things in this world are as fair as a snowfall.

Oct. 16, 24°　　　Frost crystals have grown in the night, down along the creek. They formed on the grass along the icy edge of the water. Each a different creation but all following the same pattern, growing out of their main stem. Such sparkling when the morning sun found them! I took John to see them a few hours later, but, alas, the frost enchantment was over. Luckily, I had tucked some crystals in my memory for safekeeping and they'll sparkle there forever. "What you see is what you get," said Annie Dillard in *Pilgrim at Tinker Creek.* She was talking about seeing:

> . . . There are lots of things to see, unwrapped gifts and free surprises. The world is fairly studded and strewn with pennies cast broadside from a generous hand. . .
> . . . if you cultivate a healthy poverty and simplicity, so that finding a penny will literally make your day, then, since the world is in fact planted with pennies, you have with your poverty bought a lifetime of days. It is that simple. What you see is what you get.

This morning's crystals were just such pennies to me.

Oct. 24, 16°　　　I spy some colorful currant leaves out behind the dog yard. When I bring them into the warm cabin, the leaves give up: too many temperature extremes. They fall on the table as we eat dinner.

Those leaves that were some of the first to open are the last to hold on.

Oct. 28, 12°　　　A fine sprinkling of snow falls this morning, looking like a sifting of powdered sugar on the land. A fragile roof of ice seals the creek, holding the snow dust and tracks of a snowshoe hare. I can still hear the creek below the ice, but I must listen more carefully to hear it now.

I fill the bird feeder and watch to see who comes first. In minutes the black-capped chickadees appear and then a few minutes later, the boreal chickadees. I neglect these neighbors during the summer, for then I'm too busy with all the exotic visitors, those fair-weather friends. Like the bare, abiding trees, the survivors of summer's fling of leaf and blossom, perhaps the chickadees love this place too much to leave.

The dees flit in, bite a sunflower seed, and flit away to a safer twig to eat. Daintily they hold the seed in their toes and nibble away. Sometimes I put out "wild bird seed" containing unhulled sunflower seeds, which the dees still prefer to everything else in the mixture. Now where in the memories of these northern birds do they know about sunflower seeds? I can't think of a native plant that has similar seed. How do they know there is something inside the striped hull? Aha, I must remember that this boreal forest is near the northern boundary of the black-cap's geographic range. Certainly in the southern parts of their range, chickadees have lived together with sunflowers for thousands of years. Do these wee birds at my feeder, these less-than-an-ounce bundles of fluff, bone, body, and brain, have this information in their genes?

I recognize some common character in both sunflower and chickadee, some essence they both radiate, which I can only name as *good cheer.* Whether I attribute to them this quality, or they give it to me, I'm not certain. Whatever, the chickadees are admirable winter neighbors and I value their companionship.

The jays find the newly supplied feeder and begin to pack away all they can cram into their beaks. They intimidate the dees, which now can only slip in between the jays' refueling runs. Suet wired to a nearby spruce trunk attracts the woodpeckers, and before the morning is over, Harry and Harriet, the hairy woodpeckers, and the downies will most likely visit. The redpolls never seem to bother with stopping at the feeder as they sing by overhead. They always seem in a hurry to be somewhere else. Occasionally they descend on the alders, hang, tweet, warble, and eat, and then, as suddenly as they landed, they are all off in a cloud of wings and song.

One lone male pine grosbeak honors my feeder every so often. I hear his springy aria and look to see his rosy, fanciful plumage, so outstanding in the winter woods. His rare visits are some of my winter's highlights.

The early morning's flurry of snow has plumped out to slow, huge, determined snowflakes. They seem to accept the end of their long descent with dignity and grace, resting together in a silent, four-inch-deep gathering. If this gathering grows all day, October will ease into November wearing splendid, sparkling robes, appropriate attire for winter's reign.

November — Welcome Winter World

Nov. 1, -4° The sky is clear and starry. This morning the young snow embraces the earth with a hug that is ten inches deep, and the land seems to blush with a new tender beauty. November's snow is here for good. There is no worry of melting by afternoon. October loved both autumn and winter; November is true to winter only.

Nov. 4, 2° Three more inches of snow overnight. Time to bring down the snowshoes from the cache. The leather thongs are still looped in a half hitch to fit my light spring boots of last April. The toe binding will have to be loosened to fit my big winter shoepacks. Old friends, these snowshoes. We have tromped many miles together. I really should take them up to the shop and paint on a new layer of varnish to protect the babiche. But I'll just go for a morning walk first. The snowshoes must want to get out and enjoy the new snow too.

My winter way of walking comes back instantly. Lifting the long webbed feet, striding with my feet wider apart than usual to keep from stepping on the inside of the snowshoes. Yes, it comes back instantly. A slower pace than walking, each step sinks down nearly to the ground, much harder than last April, when the crust on top of the snow supported my weight.

I snowshoe up the trail to the top of the old forest, weaving around two new birch trees that blew over during the summer. The sled dogs howl good-bye, but the new snow absorbs their song, making them sound miles away. Of course, this is the same place as last week, but now everything is completely new. Everything is winter. Sure there are the familiar old trees waiting along the same old sweep of the trail, but now they wait in winter robes of white, and they wait in air that is 30° cooler. They wait in a soft indirect light, with golden sparkles angling only here and there to the ground, mostly just highlighting the tops of the tallest spruce. And, yes, it is the same old me hiking up the trail, but today I walk on webbed feet and my tracks leave a herringbone pattern, and the tip of my nose is constantly cold. Now I am wearing a heavy sweater under a parka shell and warm wool mittens snug inside smoked moosehide choppers. I hold the fur cuff of my mittens on my nose to bring back the warmth. I pull the hood up on my parka to keep snow out of my neck. I can move right along, but it takes more energy to shuffle through the trillions of snowflakes gathered in my way and I work up a fair sweat. I will need that warm cabin to dry off in when I return. The rich moose stew simmering on the stove will be appreciated tonight. No summer salads for a meal in November. The winter world is different, and I am different. Welcome home, winter.

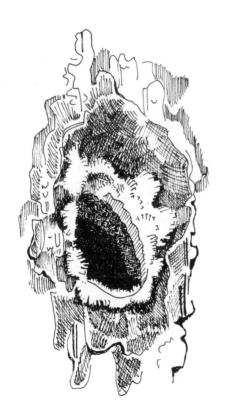

Nov. 6, 14°   Walking through the old forest, I discover a woodpecker's home in a standing, dead spruce snag. Its entrance hole, chipped out of the soft, decaying wood, is decorated with a wreath of frost flowers — intricate, crystalline accumulations of the woodpecker's breath, escaping out of the roosting tree only to freeze instantly upon meeting the cold air. I'm tempted to knock-knock to see if anyone is home, but I know my greeting would only cause alarm.

The bracket fungi growing on birch trees form little shelves holding five inches of snow — for safekeeping? For whom, this pantry of snow shelves?

Nov. 7, 6°   Winter winds from the northwest clear the branches of the recent snowload. The picnic tree, the tall spruce on the end of the knoll in front of the cabin, sounds as it it will crash over at any moment. A spiral crack begins about a foot from the ground and opens to a height of seven feet. As the wind swooshes the upper branches, the crack twists open one to two inches and then squeezes closed again.

The strength of wind testing the strength of spruce, a fair match most of the time around here, as we seldom have winds over 30 mph. I put my ear to the bark and hear what sounds like many fibers of the tree popping apart

Something is having quite a picnic on the tamarack trees, leaving lots of empty hulls on the snow beneath. No squirrel tracks to be found, so it must be a bird. I wonder which one?

Nov. 8, 0°   More snow. Four inches fell yesterday, further transforming the colored world to one of black and white. My eyes catch the five-foot-tall highbush cranberry plant on the trail to the outhouse. The branches droop from the new snow-load, yet under all this white frost, clusters of brilliant crimson berries dangle down. These berries are the only color I find in all this whiteness, and on closer inspection I find each berry is topped off with a little mountain of snow of its own.

Farther up the trail I turn back to glimpse the red again, to reassure myself that the world does indeed exist in living color. To my amazement, a Bohemian waxwing is also attracted to this flash of crimson on black and white. This harlequin bird, with the lemon-yellow wing bars on its smooth gray plumage and the waxy red spots on the tips of its secondary wing feathers, seems to ignore the rules of camouflage most winter birds survive by in this woods. This is no breeding plumage fluffed out only in springtime to assure continuation of waxwings. The Bohemians sport their bold feathers all the year round, and the only possible camouflage advantage I can imagine is that the red waxy dots match exactly the color of the cranberries. In my walking I keep an eye out for abandoned feathers. I have found quite a few, and they decorate the crack in the log near my desk. How I would love to discover a bright-yellow striped waxwing feather, or one with a spot of red wax on it.

I ponder waxwings all the way home, and on return I look up "Bohemian" in my dictionary and find "An artist or writer who disregards conventional standards of behavior." Well named, O Waxwing, and thanks for a bit of color on a snow-white day.

Nov. 10, -7°   A flurry of chickadees appears with the first faint hint of morning light. Perhaps the hours of kerosene lamplight in the dark beckon them in. Each in turn flit-flits by the bird feeder hanging in front of the window by my desk. They check out the dangling, carved-out coconut shell, looking to see if I've filled it with sunflower seeds yet. These small neighbors help keep me on schedule.

I open the glass jar in the pantry and fish out a handful of seeds. I walk around back, keeping close to the cabin, hoping not to attract the jays. If they see me they will move in and the chickadees will have to wait their turn. Today I put the seeds in the shell and stand quietly nearby. The dees sail in one at a time, take a seed, and retreat to a nearby alder to eat. The black-caps seem most confident, but the boreal chickadees take their turn, waiting in a holding pattern until just the right moment. Without my parka I soon become chilled and return to my desk on the other side of the window. For the next several hours the dees will come and go, and I will look up from my writing and enjoy their company.

Nov. 13, -5°   Snowshoed down through the forest, across the burn, and ended up out on the dog trail, which looped home. On a turn in the dog trail I was startled by a row of single wolf tracks and a bright-yellow urine stain in the snow. I scooped up some of the yellow snow and sniffed it. Even my weak nose could detect the wolf scent. For the first few seconds I was frightened. Then my knowledge that wolves do not lie in wait for people and, indeed, want as little to do with people as possible, took control, and I followed the tracks around the corner and down the valley. A ways farther down the trail another set of tracks appeared. The second wolf stepped exactly in the same holes the trailbreaker wolf had left. In a small clearing the second wolf passed the first and took a turn out in front. Near the corner where the trail turns back toward the cabin, they changed their gait from a trot to a lope. Did they hear the sled dogs or smell the woodsmoke?

In the afternoon I ran the dogs down-valley and found possibly the same tracks coming and going along the trail for eight miles to the east. Nice to have wild visitors in the valley. If the dogs howl tonight, I'll hurry out to listen for an answer.

Nov. 15, 19°   As I write at my little birch desk, a kerosene lamp on either side of me, I can't help looking up to watch the sunrise on the south-facing slope above the cabin. At about 10:30 the cold blue-white light first softens with a little rosy warmth. As the color slides down the hill, it intensifies to a salmony orange and then, yes, an honest, here-we-go-again yellow white. Out of the blue, the most vibrant, basic blue, comes another day. What a gift! Not to be taken for granted. How quickly the days pass.

Time is what life is made of, and today is the only certainty I have.

I resist the urge to chase after the sunlight and force myself to stay at my desk, working out these words I want to share with others.

At exactly 12 noon the sun strikes in between the tall spruce, illuminating the cabin with a golden radiance which can't be ignored. The sun is only a few degrees above the ridge to the south. In another hour and a half it will disappear below that ridge. The forest will remain lit with indirect lighting until about 4:00 when the long dusking begins. By 5:00 there is not enough light to see what you're doing. Officially we have only six hours and 29 minutes of daylight, losing six to seven minutes each day. In another week the sun will find this southern ridge too high to climb. The gears of earth and sun continue to mesh, and as the earth tilts back away from its own star, the angle of light decreases, a simple fact everyone learns in third grade. But the implications of this fact are greater and rule the world here in the North. Here they are not so readily overlooked.

The low sun of winter not only gives little light but also little heat. Without enough heat, water in plants freezes, and without water flowing through plants, photosynthesis can't continue. Northern plants close down for the winter. They enter dormancy, a patient life-style, but a necessary one for remaining alive until next April. Then the returning spring sun and heat will draw up the sap, and the tree will begin again. The pattern of annual rings on a tree stump reflects this life of alternating waiting and growing, as the earth wheels around the sun.

We long for answers, reasons, and systems that explain the world around us. Some find that God or good or nature or science is the way. I can't say any one answer is enough, but the questions are beautiful, and wondering is worthwhile. There is contentment in searching for your own answer.

Some animals hole up for winter, much like the plants. Insects not only change life-style, they also change life-form. Moths and butterflies are snug as a bug in a rug, or, I should say, as a larva in a cocoon.

Tiny wood frogs have rustled down under the leaves and mud to wait out the next nine months. Wood frogs cram in a lot of living in the three months of sunshine.

Now the bird's-eye view of the world enjoys an elevated perspective. Some birds are better off staying home here in the North for the winter. These are the species who over evolutionary time have acquired adaptations for coping with darkness and cold weather. But they are not many. I can name the winter residents on two hands: boreal chickadee, black-capped chickadee, gray jay, raven, hairy woodpecker, downy woodpecker, black-backed woodpecker, Northern three-toed woodpecker, common redpoll, hoary redpoll, pine grosbeak, white-winged crossbill, Bohemian waxwing, Northern shrike, great horned owl, great gray owl, boreal owl, hawk owl, goshawk, spruce grouse, ruffed grouse, sharp-tailed grouse, willow ptarmigan, rock ptarmigan, white-tailed ptarmigan, occasionally the tiny brown creeper, and the flashy magpie. (Well, maybe I can count them on two hands and two feet, and with a little help from a friend.) Sounds like a lot, but to count the summer visitors I'd need to count on the feet of several centipedes. These avian tourists court, nest, and raise their young under the northern summer sun, but in late August they use their built-in flight passes to follow the warm rays south.

The hardy sourdough birds that remain here all year round have various ways to survive the winter. Some species switch to a vegetarian diet, choosing seeds, needles, and buds, in lieu of the abundant insects and fish favored by many summer birds. The sourdoughs also have dense, downy feathers for excellent insulation from the cold. As the temperature drops, the down fluffs up, trapping more warm body heat around the bird. Woodpeckers, creepers, and chickadees roost in standing snags where their body heat is conserved inside the hollowed-out trunks. Grouse and ptarmigan dive deep into the snow and let that white blanket keep them warm.

This morning our friend, also named John, comes by for a visit. John is an enthusiastic biologist, always willing to try to answer questions. We talk about the visitors to the bird feeder as we sip coffee and I ask, "How are these Alaskan birds different from the birds that live in warmer climates?"

John nods his head as he answers, "I've done some reading on this, and these northern birds do have some neat adaptations to the cold. For example, they have more feathers, they have very little skin exposed, and they have legs that are tendonous rather than muscular. Birds' blood chemistry is impressive: they have a high concentration of glucose, almost double that of humans. This increases their metabolism. They also shiver, which helps generate heat."

"Northern birds have a different circulatory system in their exposed legs. The arteries and veins are closer together so the warmer blood traveling away from the heart reheats the cooler blood returning."

"Redpolls are able to tolerate the coldest temperatures. They have a special pouch in their esophagus where they store food, which is digested throughout the night. And, of course, you know about clumping?"

"Clumping," I repeated, "what's clumping?"

John continued, "Well, we've found that some birds, like brown creepers, huddle together, sitting very still. This shares their body heat, passing it out to their neighbors, rather than just radiating it out into the air."

"That's just what sled dog puppies try to do," I add. "They prefer sleeping all piled on top of each other. When they're about four months old, they still try to cram into a doghouse together, but they just don't fit any more."

Nov. 19, 2°   As I tramp through the woods, I always move systematically toward the sunny stretches. Now I have been out for nearly two hours and those sunny stretches are gone. The sun has rolled down below the ridge and I return home in gray light. A flutter of chickadees centers around the bird feeder. They announce my arrival with their bright calls. Earth around the sun, chickadees around the feeder, life rolls on. The promise of this morning's long sunrise has been fulfilled.

Nov. 23, -7°   The waning moon rises in the east a little later each night. No matter, the moon is always welcome. Overhead, the Dipper pours out in a clockwise swirl. The handle is in a new position each time I go out, but the North Star remains true.

I'm comforted by standing near the big spruce trees in front of the cabin. Their 80- to 90-foot trunks tilt together toward the top, encircling me. It is good to stand here, alone in the dark, again in the confidence of stars. Which three were those I first saw in August, when I wished for an early cold and deep snow? Cares get lost in the space between the tops of the spruce and the closest stars. I wonder where the chickadees are tonight? Do they dream of tomorrow's sunrise?

Nov. 24, -3°   Out on the burn I pass a particularly favorite tamarack tree. From about five feet up to eight feet, the branches have all been snapped off, leaving one- to two-inch knobs. The bark is scraped off for a foot on opposite sides of the trunk about six feet high.

Something about this spot must have appealed to a bull moose during the rut last month, and this was his rubbing tree. It seems a good location, just below a draw and just above a widening valley. I'll keep an eye on this tree, see if he uses it again next fall. I think the tamarack will survive just fine. I wish I had seen him raking his antlers and rubbing his forehead against the tree.

Nov. 26, -19°   Friends from town come out for Thanksgiving. Some ski out; others dog sled. We all meet on the trail and share the fresh doughnuts I keep warm in the sled bag. Hot water from Thermos bottles provides tea and cocoa.

I give thanks most days, for my own life and for those I love, for this wonder-full world and the opportunity to know it intimately. But the Thanksgiving celebration adds the joy of friendship and sharing. Everyone brings part of the meal — a homegrown turkey, some winter squash from Gail's garden, some honey from Eric's own bees, pickled carrots from Pete, pie crust made with real black bear grease, a gift from Bill and Fronzie. A great celebration. Relatives are far away so we adopt friends to round out the family. Before we eat, we join hands and sing the old Shaker tune:

> *'Tis a gift to be simple,*
> *'Tis a gift to be free,*
> *'Tis a gift to come down where we ought to be,*
> *And when we are in the place just right,*
> *We will be in the valley of love and delight.*

I give thanks for friends who are near and families who are near in heart.

Nov. 29, -24°   Beneath the insulating blanket of snow, the earth breathes steadily. At the base of some tree trunks, this breath surfaces and is captured in frost. Each day the frost-feathers grow thicker, extending their central axes. Down along the creek, thousands of crystals cover entire black spruce trees, ten feet tall. The sun never shines in this steep valley any more. Here the frost-feathers have bloomed in little bouquets, with some individual crystals reaching four to six inches.

I make my way through the spruce, brushing against the crystal-covered branches, shattering the delicate constructions. The flakes of ice scatter and clatter, sounding for all the world like tiny plates of glass disintegrating.

Nov. 30, -30°   Winter smoke swirls up from the stovepipe — the home fire keeps a-burning. This third of the year holds the "ember" months, the months with the longest names to tumble off your tongue. What's in a name? Amber-September, Sober-October, Remember-November, and Limber-December? Will the earth roll over in December?

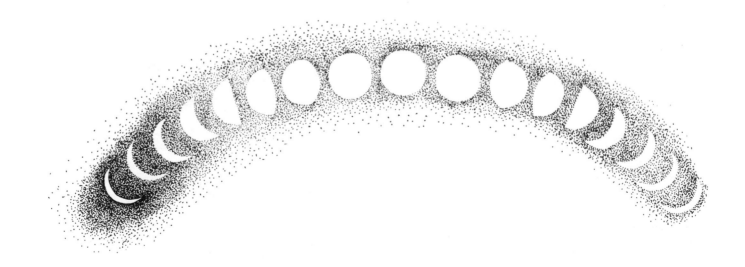

57

"In a dear-nighted December. . . " (John Keats)

Dec. 2, -24°   This afternoon as I split firewood on the chopping block in front of the cabin, I notice two boreal chickadees poised motionlessly on the moose-antler bird feeder. They are absolutely still, as if under a spell. Searching for a hint of life, I am relieved to see the breast feathers puffing up and down very rapidly.

Are they sleeping? No, a dark eye blinks. Are they frozen in fear of some predator? I see no threat.

After two minutes the pair suddenly wakes up and casually continues pecking at the suet, as if released from the spell, or refreshed after a nap. Perhaps there is some secret game of "Captain May I?" being played in this woods and the Captain was looking this way for movement. I continue my wood-splitting step, contemplating the identity of the Captain and the scope of the game.

Dec. 9, -17°   By 9:30 there is light enough to see outside. The sun never peeks over the ridge to the south, but its rays reach up to the top of the ridge north of the cabin, melting the crest with a golden-pink glow. I am warmed by this miracle every day. There is light enough to carry on.

The light is indirect, an even, overall light, like on a cloudy day — but no yellow — no shadows. I go about my day, knowing this half-light has its time, that the golden rays will return. I can be content waiting in the earth's shadow for a month, but when I run the dogs out the trail east of this valley, into the golden light, I am invigorated by its power. Hoarfrost accumulation on the branches catches the sun and the individual crystals sparkle back like a thousand diamonds.

Without this month of twilight I could never realize this amazing joy of streaming out into the sunshine. Nor would I know the subtle beauty of "dear-nighted December," as John Keats put it.

Dec. 11, -24°   The sky holds calm colors this time of year. Baby blue with tender-pink underlit billowy clouds. Most of the daylight is either part of dawn or dusk, and the sky always keeps me aware of time.

Dec. 12, -25°   Walked out to the burn to watch the sunset tonight. Normally I face the western sky's last glow, but tonight I also look back at the eastern sky, to watch the shades of darkness quiet the day. Tonight is a celebration of the night and the dark. I will wait for the slim crescent moon easing up in the southeast. This silver sliver is so low in the sky that I will only catch it a short time. After the past weeks without the full-moon brightness, I have gotten used to the dark sky again. The snow reflects some starlight and even this is brighter than the nights of September before the snow came. I need about 15 minutes for my eyes to adjust and then I can manage quite well. My only fear is being poked in the eye by a branch.

I am not alone out here in the dark. There are creatures that wait all day snuggled up in hollow trees or under the thick branches at the bases of spruce trees. They wait for the protection of the darkness to come out and feed. The hunters also wait. They use the same darkness to stalk their prey. The same night that hides the hunted also hides the hunter. I have seldom witnessed this everyday occurrence of predation. I see the story in the snow the next morning and search for clues to solve each mystery.

I will make an effort this winter to know better the night. I admit I am a diurnal creature; the sunlight allows my life by making the first green leaves. And sunlight always feels most comfortable. But the night is not darkness from sunset to sunrise. The qualities of the black sky change throughout the night.

On several long-distance dogsled races, I have traveled throughout the night and been surrounded by the darkness out on the trail. Riding the runners of a dogsled, slipping on the mile-wide frozen Yukon River, I enjoyed a sensational view of the night. One feels insignificant compared to the immensity of the sky and the multitude of stars. Insignificant, yet also comfortably at home. I always feel a bit relieved when the first pale glow grows in the southeast. I am a creature of the day, but I always feel an advantage, a wholeness, for having known the night. Somehow I am better prepared to know the day, for they are both complements of each other.

Dec. 15, -20°   The creeks are overflowing again. Our home creek, a modest spring-fed creek flowing underground much of its route, is small enough in the summer to step across with your eyes shut. The dog trail has compacted the snow where the trail crosses, damming up the main channel. The water spreads out horizontally, oozes up over the ice, and overflows. Now the stretch of ice is 20 feet wide and by spring this will certainly expand. Walking up the ice, I can find the very edge where the water is slowly creeping down the ice. The cold air freezes the water quickly, and only the leading finger flows fluidly. With changes in the temperature, the overflow changes in character. Some days there are several inches of water-slush on top of the ice. Some days I can barely walk on the slick surface, slipping constantly. Other days, the ice has enough texture to walk easily.

The growing ice provides great opportunities for the snowshoe hares. The ice lifts them up to reach the willows along the creek that have hung just out of reach all summer. Sometimes the ice traps the tips of the snow-laden shrubs, freezing them arched over for the winter. Not only can the hares dine on the new growth at the tops of the willows, but they also enjoy the cover the tunnels beneath provide. Under the willows the hares can eat and rest and be fairly safe from the great horned owls.

Almost every night I hear the owls booming out over the creek valley. I imagine a hundred snowshoe hares freezing in their tracks, beneath the willows. Their hearts pound under all that white fur. I feel the owl eyes watching me, waiting for my steps to flush a young, panicked hare. I can almost hear him turn his head over his shoulder, blink his great golden eyes, ruffle his feathers, and then fall backwards off the branch and dive to some other shadow. Tonight I can hear all of it — and my own squeaky footsteps on the cold snow, returning to the cabin, one creature enjoying the fine, cold winter night.

Dec. 16, -15°   Today I gathered spruce boughs for a Christmas wreath. Over Thanksgiving a musher took off with dogs too eager for him to control, and in his wake, a fairly good-sized black spruce was broken off along the trail. These branches will be full and just the right length for the wreath.

As I salvaged the boughs, I heard a loud crack from across the creek. Instinctively I looked up, just in time to watch a huge old birch tree heave into the branches of the neighboring trees. It rested there about ten seconds and then continued down, gaining momentum once the balance point was passed. The heavy trunk bounced once, twice, the bark splitting and cracking. The snow-covered ground shook for an instant and then accepted its new load.

So, I have watched the tiny young birch shoots rise up out of the earth (does the earth shake then also?) and followed their progress over the years. Now I witness the death of a mature tree, a death by old age. The suddenness startles me, but then that is death's way.

I make my way over to the fallen birch and examine it respectfully. At the base, where the trunk is snapped apart, the core of the tree is soft and moist. Heart rot is the official cause of death. This is the same in most of the birch fallen in the past ten years. These birch are over-mature; they have passed their normal life expectancy of 120 years. The forest is passing into a white spruce stage. Around the cabin we have lost 20-30 trees, most of which were birch. I will return here from time to time on my walks.

The death of this tree began some years ago, when the inner rot took hold. Now the long, slow process of decay will return the tree to the soil. Insects, molds, and fungi will break down the fibers of wood. With cool soil temperatures year round, decomposition will progress slowly. I'll watch for new seedlings to appear in the sunlight now available where the shade of the tree had covered the forest floor. Little new soil has been exposed, so perhaps the only change will be in the plants already growing here. Perhaps the moose will come and strip the upper branches, as they have done on many other downed birch. The shelter of the thick branches may provide cover for hares, squirrels, voles, shrews, and many birds. The resistant birch bark will offer a safe tunnel long after the wood has rotted away and the moss has overgrown it. This birch has passed from one stage of life to another. Life will go on here forever. A tree fell in the woods and I was there to hear it fall, see it fall. Now I feel closer to the spirit of the woods, the spirit of life, which also includes death.

Dec. 18, 25°   Walked right out to the outhouse without my parka on, and never felt cold. In fact, I felt overwhelmed by the moist, warm air. Just two days ago, the temperature was -15°. That's a 40° change, the difference between autumn and winter, winter and spring. Ropes of snow loop down and along the alder branches. I spoonerize their substance and call them "flow snakes." I'll take advantage of the warm weather to do some cold chores.

The sled dogs smell sweet, like the hay in their doghouses. The dog yard smells not-so-sweet due to the winter's accumulation of urine. When I smell where a red fox has marked his territory along the trail, I am happy for my sniffer, grateful to be let in on this secret of the wild ones. But, when I wind the dog yard, where 11 canines have been marking their territories, enough is too much. (Thank goodness the solids have been removed daily!)

The warm air adds a whole new dimension to life. On my walk I concentrate on smelling everything that's out there. Instead of birds sighted, or songs heard, I'll go for *fragrances smelled*. Two hours later, here's my "Nose Knows List":

1. spruce pitch on trunk of tree
2. dropped spruce needles under tree
3. green spruce needles on the branch
4. birch firewood, drying in the woodshed
5. smell of soil along creek banks, the same minerally smell of the moose lick in the summer
6. fox scent on corner of trail
7. woodsmoke from the cookstove; sweet birch smoke sinks into the valley below the cabin
8. fishmeal in the dog food barrels
9. suet on the birdfeeder
10. smoked moosehide of my mittens
11. birch resins from the little white bumps on the saplings

Well, that's a beginning. I'll keep smelling as the temperature drops and see what I can add to the list in the cooler weather. If my insensitive nose enjoys this news, imagine what the wild creatures must be detecting. I admire their ability to "nose."

Dec. 19, 7°   On the first trip outside this morning, I am instantly aware of the high winds blowing over the ridge behind the cabin. All is calm in the forest around home, but the high winds signal a change coming. I return with an armful of firewood and a heartful of anticipation.

Dec. 20, 3°   The weather from the south has turned around and gone back where it came from. Radio says a cold front from our western neighbor is heading our way.

Dec. 21, -24°   _Winter Solstice._ Well, the weatherman was right. This morning the sky is absolutely clear. The air is still and brittle, and the temperature is still going down. Fine frost crystals sparkle in the air.

   To celebrate the Solstice, John and I return to the top of the ridge, about eight miles west and 1600 feet higher than the cabin. I was there on the other side of the round year, on the Summer Solstice, June 21st. We take about an hour to get there with the dog teams. The last three miles are all uphill, most of it pretty steep. But, oh, the view from the top is worth every step of the climb. We are a little sweaty from running behind the sleds. Even going uphill the dogs can pull a little faster than is comfortable to run along with. Our hoods are thrown back and our parka zippers are down. On top, the wind is blowing out of the northwest. The wind almost always blows up here. We zip up our parkas and flip up our hoods. Some peppermint tea from the Thermos tastes good with smoked salmon strips made from last summer's catch. Cranberry muffins are still warm, wrapped carefully in my sweater in the sled bag. The cranberries came from this very ridge. What wonderful little symbols of the sun to help in our celebration today.

   The southern sky is aglow with a soft rosy blush. Any minute Old Sol will ease up over the horizon. Slowly, slowly, here he comes. The snow crystals around us sparkle back a million-trillion minute sunrises. John and I and the dogs seem to be transformed by the pink glow.

   There is an Eskimo tradition in the Far North that teaches people to throw back their hoods and shake off their mittens the very moment they see the sun return. If the sun sees your bare face and hands at this time, it will bring you good luck for the year to come. We enjoy our picnic and carefully watch the sun reaching its highest arc over the ridge to the south. At that very moment, we follow the Eskimo custom and, removing hoods and mittens, try hard to feel some warmth on our faces and hands. Through our squinty eyes and frosty eyelashes, the sun radiates out in brilliant prismed rainbows. After a few freezing minutes on this cold, windy ridge, we return to our hoods and mittens. The sun rolls downhill to the southwest, seeming to gain momentum as it descends. Limber-December also rolls over and tomorrow the earth begins the slow climb back toward the high summer sun.

We suddenly realize we are very cold. We bundle up, pack up the lunch, and turn the teams back down the ridge trail. We are quiet all the way down, except for stern commands to keep the dogs slow enough to negotiate the steep trail.

Dec. 23, -14°   New snow. John will dog sled into town to check the mail, pick up Christmas supplies, and take care of a long list of errands. The dog trail stretches about 27 miles into Goldstream Valley, an area ten miles northwest of Fairbanks. There, our frozen truck waits for someone to bring it back to life. The white '63 pickup is a good runner. Even at 30° below, the motor will turn over and start on the third try.

The trail to the truck will be a slow, cold one for John. Four inches of new snow fell during the night. He'll probably take two and a half or three hours if all goes well. I pack the leftover pancakes, rolled up with jam, for a trail snack and fill his Thermos bottle with hot water. I tuck two bullion packages in the cup before I screw it on tightly. I have been careful to dry the cup and spout so no water remains to freeze it shut enroute. It is 8:30 a.m. and the sky will be dark for at least another hour and a half. Then there will be a long sunrise on the trail.

John packs the sled while I harness six huskies. The dogs are eager to stretch into a trot, and those left in the dog yard voice their disappointment. John and I hug and say good-bye, being careful to kiss quietly. On several other occasions, the eager team had mistaken our smack for the click of a tongue, a signal to take off.

As John passes me, he quietly says, "I love you."

"Have a good trip to town! Stay warm! I'll miss you!" I holler down the trail. The dogs steam down the slope, skirting the western edge of the knoll, and then curve into the black spruce. John disappears. The dogs left at home howl their good-bye and then, all at the exact same moment, fall silent. We all listen to John's sled skittering over the ice on the creek. One more brief mournful howl and the dogs sit quietly again, sharp ears following the team's progress down the valley.

I turn back toward the cabin. The kerosene lamps spill out light on the fresh snow. The two runners of the sled cut a clean, sharp trail there. I step on the tracks and somehow feel connected to John, who is by now over a mile away. This ribbon of tracks will roll out the trail, and all the time John is in town, I'll step on the tracks each time I pass near them and feel close to him.

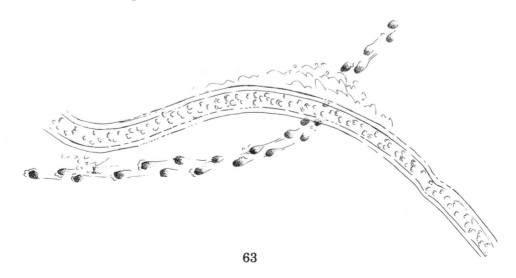

Dec. 24, -32°   I suppose that in town today many people are panicked with last-minute Christmas shopping. I can think of nothing nicer for a gift than the presence of friends. Tomorrow some of our friends will join us and we will walk the woods, sharing our time and the beautiful forest. Sharing our love of nature is such a basic common ground, and the most amazing thing about it is that there is no end to discovering small wonders. We can teach each other because we each sense with different talents and gifts. There are a billion more gifts waiting in the woods than anyone can ever hope to wrap up and put under a single Christmas tree. Sharing nature with good friends is the present, or presence, I enjoy most this time of year.

We will walk out along the burn and look for just the right Christmas tree. Thousands of young spruce are coming up there and an annual thinning by one tree is hardly noticed. We each have different ideas of what the perfect tree must look like. However, there are some basic qualifications we all agree on. The tree can only be about seven feet tall, with branches extending two feet from the trunk. The tree goes in a corner, so fullness on all sides is not necessary. Each year we make more ornaments, so another basic requirement is lots of branches where all the bright memories can be hung for the week.

Each of us drags the others through the deep snow to first one tree and then another. We point out the special features on each tree and make quite an issue over it, reminding ourselves of used-car dealers, or some stereotyped view of used-car dealers. When we agree on the best little tree, or when we get too cold to keep looking, whichever comes first, we join hands in a circle around the tree. We try to sing "O Tannenbaum," but we never remember the words and end up humming. Then our tradition directs the youngest of the group to strike the first blow with the ax, and each in turn, from youngest to oldest, takes a swing. We continue in order until the tree falls. Then one of the men hoists it up to his shoulder, and in single file we troop back to the cabin, caroling through the woods as we go along the trail. Those at the end of the line are always half a phrase behind the trailbreakers, and the squirrels and birds might wonder at our timing.

Back at the cabin, we fit the slim trunk into the heavy birch stand and bring the tree in to thaw out. The rich fragrance of spruce needles permeates the cabin as the branches relax. Soon the smell of popcorn is vying for top honors, and I bring out the needles and thread. John is the master popper, and the huge spruce burl bowl is quickly heaped high. Melted margarine and salt are added, designating this bowl as available for nibbling. Another smaller bowl is filled for the long chains we each make and string together in garlands for the spruce boughs. Next come the many small ornaments, most of which have been made by friends in Christmases past. The fragile blown eggs, walnut shells, and cookie-dough cut-outs are stored in old egg cartons. Lifting each ornament into the lamplight and admiring the handiwork of a friend, or remembering the year we created each one, brings back wonderful memories and is one of the great joys of the season. Last year some friends brought a box of beautiful brass clip-on candleholders and red beeswax candles to go into them. Even before we lit the candles, the tree radiated a warm glow. Once they were lit after dinner, we all gathered round to enjoy the steady brightness and to watch for smoking needles. Gifts were exchanged, and everyone helped unwrap the many presents my mother always sends. Mom's theory is "it doesn't matter so much what's in a gift, it's just important for everyone to have something to open." So, we guess at the toothpaste tubes and cans of nuts and the boxes of mints. Everybody acts as if whatever is opened is the very thing most wanted. Mom collects these things all year long, and I only hope she enjoys wrapping them up as much as we have fun sharing them with our Christmas company.

Dec. 28, -5°   Must be a late Christmas present from somewhere, this warm spell. I find it a relief to walk along with fewer layers of clothing on, a relaxation of muscles tensed against the cold. The chickadees seem to be singing more — perhaps that is their way of celebrating.

Dec. 31, 0°   Limber-December, are you ready to roll over and let January hold the top of the Wall Journal? The earth has already turned over and begun its swing back toward the sun. In the ten days since the Winter Solstice, the day has gained 17 minutes between sunrise and sunset, and this is noticeable to those who love the light and are out in the woods. People add one year to the date tomorrow. The earth just continues rolling on around the sun, re-turning to where it was 365 sunrises ago. Happy New Y_earth_!

January — "And the day star arise in your hearts. . ." (2 Peter 1:19)

<u>Jan. 1, -9°</u>   I have not been up the valley for quite a while, so this morning I harness up a small team and we head west. About a mile out the trail we come to fresh moose sign: two sets of deep holes in the snow along the trail, decorated with frequent piles of brown unshelled almonds, or so the moose droppings look to me. Willows are left dangling or raw-ended, with telltale brown leaves and twigs littering the snow underneath. The hares will enjoy these leftovers. The dogs pick up the scent, and the speed, as I ride the brake wishing to remain in some control if we run into company around the corner. But we don't, so off comes the brake and we continue up the valley.

An hour and a half later, on our return trip, about a mile from home, the dogs again pick up the fresh moose scent. Just as we make the curve to the right, my eyes catch a flash of movement on the left. There a cow and calf strike off in a zigzagging pattern, aiming for the cover of the old forest a few hundred yards up the slope. They might just as easily dash and crash in a straight line, for they certainly have the force to bowl over anything in their way. Perhaps going at the slight angles allows them to check our actions. The cow's long ears monitor us and the calf seems to concentrate on catching up with mama. With seemingly little effort, they trot through the dense willows and birch saplings, their tall legs hinging at the elbow, their knees folding up and down smartly. I am always impressed by moose mobility.

Today what strikes me most is the warm, rich colors of the moose's coats. Against the cold world of black and gray and white, the luxurious dark browns, rusts, and tans seem quite a contrast. It is as if only the moose were in focus in the picture and the background around them slightly blurred. Both moose hold the hairs along their necks erect, and this bristling impression makes them look wilder, more excited. No doubt my own look is somewhat wild and excited as the dog team, which was showing signs of being tired only a minute before, now breaks all previous records for the homestretch. Thank goodness the dogs usually stay on the trail, rather than following the moose tracks off into the brush. I look back quickly to see the moose, standing at the edge of the old forest, and even at this distance the warm colors of their coats again impress me. I hope these brown beauties stay around and I get to watch them again. Next time I plan to be on foot.

Jan. 3, -11°   Winter rainbows add to the sky show today. Not the brilliant arches of summer, but a pair of muted pink and yellow parentheses on either side of the sun; reflected ice crystals in the air. We call them *sun dogs*, a curious name, but they do accompany the sun in its walk across the sky.

Jan. 4, -16°   A boreal owl calls in the late afternoon, a long series of rapid hoots, rising in pitch toward the end. When I answer back I have difficulty sustaining so long a breath. My bird book describes the boreal's call as a "soft high-pitched bell or dropping of water," but this must be referring to the more intimate sound the owl makes. I have followed the hooting back to the owl and stood directly beneath its roosting tree. For some reason the boreal owl is not afraid of people. I wonder why? I have read of explorers walking right up to the wild owls and stroking their breast feathers. I was never so fortunate. In my experience, the owl just sat on its branch and returned my stare. At this close range, only six feet between us, I heard the owl make a soft, pinging sound. Perhaps this is what the bird book referred to. As I walked around the tree, the owl followed me with its bright eyes, swiveling its head more than 180°, and then, faster than I could be sure, it swung its gaze around from the other side. But why so tame? Boreal owls are the stuff that legends are made of.

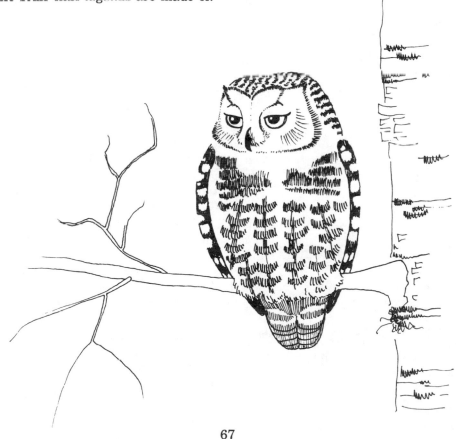

Jan. 7, -27°   The gay little Christmas tree now stands in the yard outside the front windows, looking as if it has grown there all its life. Unless you notice that it is the only young tree in acres of old forest, or you notice the birch stand sticking out solidly where the tree's roots ought to be. To the birds who know this air space by heart and claim it as their own, this new obstruction must be a surprise. All the tiny ornaments are now back in their egg-carton homes, stored up in the cache, but the popcorn garlands still cascade off the branches, this way and that, draped around the little tree. Gray jays and chickadees come a-caroling, landing in the new branches and inspecting and accepting the popcorn refreshments. The jays reign over the new territory at first, and as is their way, they try to make off with all the popcorn, bound for private stashes and caches. When I put the leftovers of the popcorn bowl out for them, the jays can do this. When we put the Christmas tree with popcorn strung together in ten-foot-long chains, this is not possible. After a few frustrating attempts to fly off with a kernel in their beaks, only to be brought back to reality by the thread holding their flight, the jays learn to perch patiently and eat where they wait.

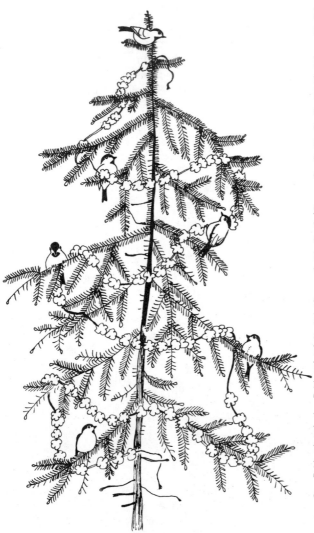

The jays are pretty to watch, all puffed up to keep warm. Like the rest of us, they finally grow full of popcorn and move off to other matters.

Seconds later a flurry of chickadees, who have been hovering in the nearby trees, swoop in and decorate the tree. They seem to understand about the thread. Did they learn by watching the jays? Both black-capped and boreal chickadees join the celebration, landing a certain, comfortable distance from each other. With four or five dees scattered on the tree, it looks like some old-fashioned Christmas card. I almost prefer this tree to the one we held captive inside last week. Our avian neighbors certainly do.

Jan. 8, -28°   Bright moon floats up over the ridge to the east. It's not quite full yet, but on a clear night like this one there is plenty of light to see. I take advantage of both moonlight and cold weather and split firewood to fill the wood rack in front of the cabin.

The wood, dry spruce and birch, is so brittle in the cold that one tap of the splitting maul shatters the log in half. In warmer weather I must strike some logs again and again. I bend, pick up a half log, balance it on the chopping block (a huge round of spruce), and split again, bend again, balance again, and split until the entire log is scattered round my feet, now in nice stove-size pieces in the snow. These I gather up and place neatly between the two side walls of the rack; spruce on the left for the cookstove and birch on the right for the heating stove. By now I am so warmed up that my parka is off and draped over the wood rack and my hat is untied under my chin. So true is Thoreau's observation that you're thrice warmed by a stick of firewood.

First you're warmed when you saw the log, second when you split the log to fit your stove, and third when you actually burn the log in the stove.

My last task is making kindling, the thin, finger-sized sticks needed for starting new fires. I save a round that is perfectly straight-grained and knot-free. I divide it down to four-inch chunks with the seven-pound maul and then switch to the lighter, sharper ax. Now the fun begins. Fun to the one person splitting; horrifying to anyone watching! I slice off thin sections, holding the sticks to be struck just beyond my fingers. I have had a few close calls but never-ever sliced my fingers. (My record slicing bread with a newly sharpened knife is much bloodier.) I try switching to gloves so I can feel the wood better, but my fingers grow cold in a few minutes and I return to the clumsy mitts. The spruce splits clear as the night, cracking off with a sound clean and final. Once a friend of mine, Mike Sager, who lives on the Yukon River, was splitting firewood in the moonlight, but this time it was during September when the moose were in the rut. Mike heard a shuffle behind him and turned to see a nicely antlered bull challenging him. The sounds of the splitting had attracted the moose, Mike concluded. Seeing as it was hunting season, and seeing as how Mike's cache was still empty, he accepted the challenge, exchanging his ax for his rifle. "Now if I had waited for the bull to go right under the cache, I would have saved myself the chore of packing him the ten feet over there," Mike always adds with a twinkle. I always think of this story when I'm splitting, and I stop every now and then to gaze out through the spruce, just in case there is a visitor.

The challenge of the kindling game is to make each stick thinner than the last stick. I tend to turn into a sorcerer's apprentice, and if that music were to come blasting out of the night, I'm sure I'd end up with a five-foot-tall pile of matchsticks — and fingers on my left hand all too short. But no music comes. The night is still in the cold. Occasionally the creek ice expands, announcing the change with a sound like a shot. Ice in the trees pops in answer, all in the slow conversation of the cold night.

A listener waiting there all night hears the whole story. I'm finished in an hour. I stand back and admire the full rack of wood and the two weeks' supply of kindling, stacked along the little porch on the other side of the door. The cabin looks so lovely in the moonlight. Knowing the cozy warmth waiting through the door, I sit on the chopping block for a few more minutes, listening to the night and the moon moving through the cold air.

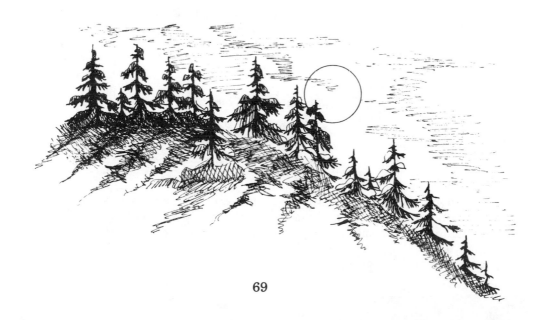

Jan. 9, -20°   Sunlight is oozing down the slope, coming closer to home each day, like a great wave reaching higher up a sandy beach.

Jan. 10, -37°   How cold will it go? In Fairbanks the temperature is down to -47°. The cold air settles in the Chena River valley, where Fairbanks sits, while up here in the hills west of town a temperature inversion is in effect, as is usual during cold weather. The warmer air, moved around by a little wind, still feels plenty cold. I'm grateful for the temperature inversion, particularly for the dogs. At -30° they often prefer to come out of their houses and just curl up on the snow. I think their breath must make it damper inside their doghouses, and therefore colder. I add lots of fat to their food and cook daily for them, so that they start out the night with a warm meal in their bellies. I shouldn't worry, for these huskies have evolved in and with the North, and they have the fur coat to take care of themselves. They curl up tightly with their noses tucked snugly in the long, furry underside of their tails. Even after the coldest nights, when I go out the next morning my old friends uncurl, shake off the frost around their ruffs, and are ready to play.

My steps squeak on the cold snow. I imagine a correlation between the pitch of that squeak and the temperature.

Jan. 13, -27°   Wolverine tracks crossing the trail at nearly the same spot as in the past three years. Good to know this wild neighbor is still making its curious rounds. I'd love to see the real creature making the tracks, but just seeing the tracks and thinking of the wolverine, the largest member of the weasel family, is thrilling.

Jan. 14, -19°   On our way up the alder chute, the steepest stretch up to the ridge, the dogs and I are entertained by the "Black Bard of the North." The raven, perched on the bare branches of a tall aspen, seems compelled to comment on our laboriously slow progress up the hill. His raucous aria, consisting of croaks and gurgles, burps, whirls, and whistles, is accompanied by the ever-present winds and seems entirely appropriate in this high country. And I suppose to one who easily gains this height with only a few wing beats, our efforts seem ridiculously inefficient. The dogs take his yodeling personally, considering it teasing, which I must say it sounds like. This teasing urges the dogs to pull even harder than they did before and quickens our climb.

When we are even with the troubadour's tree, we stop for a rest break. Raven considers this noteworthy and reports to anything out there that will listen. At this close range I can watch his marvelous antics. His gigantic black beak opening and closing, his throat, flashing iridescent black feathers, gurgling in and out as he throws his head back with the news.

I always enjoy watching ravens soar against the sky at a dark distance, but this more intimate occasion teaches me a new respect for the bird. How intelligent ravens must be to possess such a varied language. If they go to the trouble of expressing themselves so eloquently, do they know there is anyone there to listen?

Well, this particular raven knows we are listening, and I get the distinct feeling he prefers other company. He lifts off, swooping over the trail on noisy wings. We can almost feel the fanned air on our faces. The dogs chase the "wisssh-wisssh" of his wings up to the top of the first knob. Raven "roarrrks" back under his shoulder and I instinctively answer him. He dips a dark wing, loops by once more, and then dives over the ridgetop, laughing on the updraft. I laugh, too.

Jan. 16, -27° SUNSHINE IN THE TREETOPS! At high noon the highest trees around the cabin are aglow with a yellowish light. This is not the direct beam. The sun has not yet floated up above the ridge to the south, but this is the leading edge of that beam.

Jan. 18, -30° It's the real thing! Sharp golden sunshine glittering the treetops, brightening the dull green to yellow-green. This splash of sunlight brings with it all the fresh hope and glory of spring. And the day star arises in my heart!

   In about ten minutes, the gold is gone for the day, but every ending marks a new beginning, and the light will return tomorrow and tomorrow.

Jan. 21, -19° The female grouse thunders in to explore the dust and gravel under the cabin eaves. Perhaps this summer substrate in the middle of winter is a refreshing vacation for her. She pecks at the bright quartz and probably ingests some. She keeps me in view when I work around the cabin, but she doesn't seem to consider me much of a threat. We are amiable neighbors.

Jan. 25, -17° The sunlight wakes the sleeping hillsides. Color returns to the landscape in the rosy-maroon of the birch groves and the gray-green of the aspen islands. Spruce trees lose their dark tones and seem to relax into a friendlier green. Even the temperature relaxes a little. The earth and her creatures have survived another dark and cold trial.

Jan. 28, -24° While on my way out to feed the dogs, a bucket pulling low from each arm, I am almost knocked over by the flying squirrel, which glides in mid-air before my very eyes. SMACK! The squirrel hits the base of the spruce with the bird feeder hanging on it and scampers up the tree, claws a-clicking. I set my buckets down and walk close to the feeder. The light from the window is enough to let me see him, and for him to see me. The squirrel nibbles on the suet and then sits erect to observe me. He seems less nervous than the red squirrels and a little larger. After a few minutes he's had enough and pulls himself up the tree. I don't see him glide down to the other tree, but I hear him SMACK into the trunk and claw his way up to a new takeoff. What a way to fly! Squirrels that go bump in the dark are fun to run into once in a while. I pick up the two buckets and continue out to the hungry dogs, who have little patience for the squirrely delay in their dinner.

Jan. 29, -21° A wave of redpolls undulates through the forest, landing on the alders, dangling upside-down on the cones. They are a cheery crew, always singing. The joy of their singing reflects the return of sunnier days. Since the Winter Solstice we have gained about three hours between sunrise and sunset, nearly doubling the day.

Jan. 30, -22° Most amazing morning! Today I am baking, and with the cookstove oven up to temperature, the cabin is quite toasty. I open the window over the stove to let out some heat. With a fresh muffin to sample in my hand, I step out on the front porch to cool off.

   The very instant I'm out the door, a black-capped chickadee lands on my muffin! Was this an accident? Did I walk into the dee's line of flight? I freeze in my tracks. The dee flits off to the branches of the spruce directly in front of me. I stay motionless, holding the muffin in my outstretched hand up to the bird. After a minute the tiny fellow comes back to the muffin, takes another taste, and whirls away off the knoll, singing in chickadee-dee-dees as it goes.

This is the first time a chickadee has ever come to my hand. Had it been watching the camp robbers who regularly flock to a handout? I was delighted and ran up to the shop to tell John of the event. On my way back to the cabin, I noticed a black-capped on the bird feeder. I went right up to it, speaking softly, "Hello, little dee. Are you the muffin lover?" But no answer. The dee did not return to my hand. I don't even know if it was the same bird. But I am still hoping, and I'll make it a habit to taste my muffins on the front porch.

February — Northern Heartland Turning

Feb. 2, -18°   I turn the Wall Journal, gaining on the climb toward the sun. Officially the year is divided into quarters called seasons, but here in the North, white winter spreads over half of the round time. But I hear a change as I repeat the names of the months: "Jan-u-ary, Feb-ru-ary, March." The pace seems to be picking up after the heavy tumble of "Oc-to-ber, No-vem-ber, De-cem-ber." And winter seems to be passing altogether too quickly. I like seeing all the time together, all the months flowing into each other, not disappearing from my attention with the turning of a page. I like the roll from white winter into glorious green spring, around through hot yellow summer, and then suddenly, heartbreakingly beautiful amber autumn — and softly back again into winter white.

Sometimes I see myself listening with the snowy hare in December or leaping high when new brown fur tickles my nose in April. Sometimes I stretch out along the birch branches in May, easing my buds open, entwining myself with a lacework of leaves. Or I sail high with the raven, freer than the wind. Or I tunnel with the red-backed vole, whisking myself around the year.

Feb. 3, -22°   Jim Anderson hikes out today for a visit. We talk about the names of seasons and Jim shares his favorite. Beginning Feb. 1st, Jim recognizes the season of *Dazzle*, in celebration of the bright, sparkly days.

Feb. 4, -17°   Today the wind wakes up the sleepy world. I listen out by the picnic tree. How long can this bark hold the splintering inside? As I stand vertical among verticals, my eye catches a small movement on the spruce at the bottom of the knoll. The smallness of it alarms my senses. It is too small. Too small to be a chickadee, the smallest of things that moves in this forest.

And then the wee bird spirals around to my side of the trunk and I clearly see this is no chickadee. The bird creeps up and around to the right. Aha! The movement reassures me. This must be a brown creeper! The bird swoops down to the base of the tree right next to me. And I watch the creeper exploring the bark for odds and ends of summer's insect life.

Suddenly another small winged-one lands in the tree just uphill of me. Another creeper! They are dining out together! If I stand quietly enough, will one land on me and creep up around my parka? How can life survive in such tiny packages? Both creepers could easily roost in my pocket. "You're welcome, creeping wonders! If I could only understand your thin chirps, I could hear of tiny hideaways I'll never fit into, of minute ways of survival in this cold season."

Brown creepers are considered uncommon this far north. These creepers stay all year round, but they only visit the cabin occasionally. I'm lucky to be standing out in the wind, feeling like a tree rooted there, and nearly having the creepers land on me.

Feb. 8, -8°   My snowshoes tromp me out to a favorite birch stand. Those "standing" I figure to be about 40 years old, just about my own age. Forty I consider to be middle age, but for the birch, 40 is still young. The oldest birch have lived about 150 years. I pack down a little seat in the snow with my snowshoes and make myself comfortable. Interesting to visit among peers, even though I am of the animal kingdom and they represent the plant world. The white trunks are about five inches in diameter and straight as a ray of the sun. No indecision there; up that ray to the sun was the only way to grow.

The bark on the birch trunks varies considerably from tree to tree. Some trunks are smooth and clear, a dull white flecked with horizontal striations. These striations are lenticels, which allow air to enter the tree. Other trunks have wisps of papery bark fringing off in ragged curls. Still others show sheets of bark wrapping back, exposing younger, pinker bark beneath. Some parts of birches are quite gray in color. The shelf fungi which characterize the older birch are not present at this age, but the delicate gray-green lichens are already growing on the scars where lower branches have fallen away.

Here and there between the healthy trunks are the remains of older birches, just standing dead snags now. As the forest matured, many of the trees, probably the majority of the trees, were thinned out as saplings. Snowshoe hares might have pruned many of them, leaving sharp, clean stumps. But that was at least 20 years ago, and most of those trunks have rotted away by now. I have visited this grove for over 14 years, and I remember those hare-clipped stumps that still stood when I first came.

Feb. 9, -12°   Tonight a ring of snow crystals around the moon, a halo of soft pink and yellow. Will the warm clouds shake down some snow?

Feb. 14, -8°   Today, on the day of hearts, I remember valentines of the past. These hearts come in all seasons. Once I ventured north to the arctic coast of Alaska, near Point Barrow. The season was spring and the month was May. Female snowy owls sat on their nests to protect their eggs from the cold north wind. Their nests were shallow depressions on the tops of hummocks, two or three feet higher than the surrounding tundra. The owls slowly swiveled their heads, and their great golden eyes stared off for miles in each direction. The wind ruffled their white feathers, which were dappled with brown to help camouflage the owls as the snow melted. One day I found a snowy owl feather. It was all white except for one perfect brown heart. I think it was a valentine from the birds.

In summer of another year, I found a smooth, dark stone under the clear waters of a mountain stream. In the very center of the stone was a white quartz heart. This was no artifact, no crafting of man. This was a valentine from the mountains.

Yet another year, I was gathering cranberries on a frosty morning in early September. The aspen leaves had turned golden overnight, except for one single tree that shivered in crimson. On the ground below that tree were a hundred fragile leaf hearts — valentines from the forest.

Now the season is winter and it is my turn to pass on these valentines. There is a love in this earth we must return, and then pass on.

Feb. 18, -6°   Two ravens twirl-dive down the warm, blue sky, looping and swooping, squawking and hawking their joy. Is it the joy of warmer temperatures or brighter days or the urge to breed again with their lifelong mates? I croak up to them, but they are consumed with their aerial acrobatics and pay me no mind. But I share their exuberance. I also breathe this new air saturated with spring fever.

Feb. 24, -8°   The frost line is melting down the hillside. The upper third of the slope is defrosted, with bright twigs shimmering in maroon and green. The lower two-thirds of the hill is still softened by white branches, stubborn crystals clinging until the warm rays make clean contact.

Feb. 26, -5°   In celebration of the fine weather, I take off with the dog team for a little overnight camping trip. On the way up the ridge, I peel off the upper layers as the ascent steepens. First off comes the hat and gloves, next the parka, and then the heavy sweater and one wool shirt. Woolly dogs can only pant and roll in the snow during rest breaks to cool themselves off.

Willow buds have fluffed out up here, helping to distinguish the different willows. I will try to remember to take a branch home for John tomorrow when I return this way.

On top of the first ridge the trail snakes along the crest for a few miles. A swarm of 40 or 50 white-winged crossbills escorts us along our way, weaving themselves together and then apart and then together again, a dull red-and-yellow undulation of wing beats. In unison they swirl back toward us, seemingly impatient with our earthbound pace, yet curious about our invasion of *their* ridgetop. All the while they're carrying on their high-speed maneuvers, the cheery birds are whistling at various pitches. They remind me of tiny varied thrushes, singing in proportion to their size.

A fresh marten track catches my eye. Such a simple pattern, the two footprints almost side by side, angling through the alpine forest. We are close to the top of the ridge, which takes us just up above treeline. The trees here are white spruce, but they are stunted, I suppose by the constant wind which has scoured their lower branches. I wonder what the marten finds to eat up here? An occasional red squirrel in the spruce, and a very few snowshoe hares, from the looks of the tracks. Martens normally eat mice, voles, and shrews, but this is not the place to find them. Often I find ptarmigan tracks up here, but I think ptarmigan are too big for the marten to take on. Perhaps the marten is out celebrating the fine weather, too.

I tie the sled off at the last tree and hike up to the rock outcrop. Amazingly, the wind is absent, a rare treat up here. I eat my lunch in a nook in the rocks. The brown surface appears warm but gives no radiant heat. I remember my April visit here, but I'll have to wait a while before geese fly over again.

I return to the dogs and we shoot up and over the crest of the ridge. Now the exciting trip down the other side has me clinging tightly to the steering bow. The dogs are responsive to my "easy now" command, and I ride the brake to slow us even more. We'll drop 2000 feet in less than two miles, so I'll have to enjoy the view as it blurs by. I feel I am about at my limit in controlling the sled and I pray we don't run into a moose. We never have seen one up here, but the dogs often wind them and take chase for short spurts. We sail down the wind-packed alpine terrain. The hard waves of snow provide excellent footing for the dogs. A little farther down we pass through some open-growing spruce, a few straggly birch, and then a zone of pure spruce. This gives way to a magic grove of aspen holding down a little knob. The aspen are all contorted by the wind. The trunks are large and solid, and altogether too close to the trail. The sled grazes along them on the downhill side. Abruptly the aspen are left behind and we coast into a pure birch stand. The open, light feeling is comforting, as is the leveling pitch of the trail. After half a mile of birch, we again move into spruce, huge white spruce, with an understory of alder. The alders bend low over the trail, forcing me to crouch behind the sled. The trail follows out along a hogback where I am delighted to stand up again, surrounded by giant old cottonwoods. The rough gray bark is friendly, and the sunlight streams through the bare branches. At last we pull into our old camp. A pile of dry firewood still waits under the branches of a big spruce and is fairly free of snow. I unharness the dogs and gather some more firewood. The sun is just about to go down, and the temperature is dropping. I collect several armfuls of spruce boughs, cutting a few from many different trees. I arrange them for a bed between two spruce next to the firewood. I feed the dogs and start the campfire. The flames reassure me. The smoke brings warm memories. I roll out my caribou hide on top of the spruce boughs and sled tarp. Dinner will be simple: macaroni and cheese, and a cup of hot chocolate. The snow melts to water quickly and the hot drink tastes wonderful. After dinner I keep the fire going a little while and then turn in, cozy in my fluffy sleeping bag. It's only about eight o'clock but I am weary. The fire burns down quickly and the dark shadows subdue the last embers. It's easy to be scared if you let your imagination take control. I reassure myself and say good night to my good dogs.

The thick spruce mattress is quite comfortable and I feel no cold from the snow beneath me. I miss John by my side. He is home, working in the shop on a woodworking project. He is an artist with wood and he loves his art. When we camp together, much of my attention is on John. Being alone tonight creates an entirely different feeling: a solitary person, stretched out on a few feet of the earth, peeking up at a billion stars only a million miles away. Life is so simple.

Somewhere out on the flats to the west a wolf howls, and the sled dogs immediately answer. I snuggle down in my sleeping bag, a smile on my face and the sweet relaxation of sleep soothing my tired body.

A busy chirping and whistling awakens me. I peer out of my sleeping bag and see two gray jays checking out my camp in the first light of morning. A little frozen macaroni and cheese left on my dinner plate seems to be what they are excited about. They tilt their head and look at me first from one side and then the other. Last year when I camped here, three jays joined me for breakfast. I wonder if these are some of the same? I pull on my clothes and stuff my feet into frozen boots. (Again I miss John, for he always gets up first and starts the fire before I venture out of my warm nest.) A little birch bark with dry spruce twigs on top ignites quickly with only two matches, and soon the sweet smoke is drifting out through the trees. I make the rounds of the sled dogs. They each stretch and shake off the night's frost and lean into me when I give them a good-morning pat. I check the thermometer on the sled: -10°, not bad. With the sun up for another few hours, we'll see zero by noon. Is it possible to see nothing?!?

I melt snow for coffee and make some oatmeal. The bag of frozen cranberries is added, and I wait for them to melt in the heat of the oatmeal. I toast the frozen muffins near the fire so I can bite into them without breaking off my front teeth. I should have sliced them at home before they froze. I throw bits of muffin toward the jays waiting in the branches, and they waste no time joining the picnic. They act just like the jays of last year, so tame, so confident. The jays clean up the crumbs and disappear into the forest.

After too many cups of coffee, I break camp and pack the sled. We'll take a loop trail out across the lakes and then head home, back over the ridge. Going up the trail on this side will be much slower today, and I will be able to enjoy the changing forests. Counting the black spruce section, which stretched below my camp and out to the lakes, this trail enjoys all the tree species of the Interior except for tamarack. I shall have to explore for tamarack and then reroute the trail to make it arboreally complete.

The daylight now stretches from about six in the morning to six in the evening, including the long, slow dawn and dusk. The glorious molten colors remind me of the hope and promise, the peace and contentment life offers. I feel the pace of the earth picking up as we turn higher toward the summer sun. Cold weather will be with us a few months longer, but an unmistakable spring essence is present. On the way up the ridge, I propose a new season: "winter-spring." The land is held by winter, but the day star promises spring. This best of both worlds swells the heart and soars the spirit.

March — Into Winter-Spring!

March 3, 8°   I am intoxicated again. The bright, windy March weather always treats me this way. My restless spirit longs to wander, to watch the winter world shake loose and yawn and stretch like a husky sled dog in the morning. The land and the living insist on celebrating. We have lived with the challenges of the cold and the dark; now all we can do is smile back at the sun.

March 4, 7°   The gray jays are still courting and some of them are already building nests. They boldly hop around in the dog yard, tilting their heads, looking first from one eye and then the other. They are looking for dog fur, and when they spy a tuft, they snatch it in their beaks and cruise off to some secret nesting site. How warm those three to five spotted, gray-green eggs will be with the woolly fleece below them and the mother jay settled on top, her bare brood patch directly over the eggs, her fluffy down feathers all around them. I am finding the charcoal down feathers on the snow again — perhaps a molt related to breeding?

March 5, -4°   Last night, while enjoying a late walk, I suddenly stopped to listen carefully. Yes, I heard the eerie, high-pitched scream again. Lynx are breeding now, and the scream was a wild exaggeration of a domestic cat's lament. I listened a while longer, but the concert was over.

March 7, 2°   The creek is overflowing again, the water adventuring out the dog trail some 60 feet from the actual summer channel. So much ice from this little creek! I am continually amazed. But perhaps my thinking is backwards. Perhaps in the north, where winter rules for more than half the year, this icy form is the real character of the creek. The watery stage of summer may just be the dormant time, before the growth of winter. What did Carl Sandburg ask in "Metamorphosis"?

> *When water turns to ice does it remember*
> *one time it was water?*
> *When ice turns back into water does it*
> *remember it was ice?*

The overflow spreads out on the trail, making a safe crossing nearly impossible with a fresh team. Today I cut an alternative trail a ways downstream, and on my way back over the new route I discover a bird's nest I must have dislodged during trail cutting. The nest is perfect: a three-inch-deep cup of about the same width. The lower two inches are woven twigs and grass; the upper inch a swirl of gray-green horsetails topped with soft, dry, green moss. What to do? Could I return the nest to a satisfactory nook in the alder so the rightful owner could use it again this spring? I should try, but instead I bring the treasure back to the cabin. Easter is coming soon and I will place some sweet, dry rosebuds in the nest for eggs and hide it away in a friend's home. This friend is a carver of wooden bowls and he will appreciate this perfectly crafted bowl for birds' eggs.

March 12, 12°   The tangy odor of fox urine is pungent along the trail. The warmer air carries the smell better. Foxes are mating now and this no doubt calls for more advertising.

March 13, 26°   After two days of this balmy weather, I am startled by monster tracks that have appeared in the burn. Gigantic hares have thumped over the snow, leaving tracks nearly one and a half feet long! Normally, the prints are only about a third this size. At first I thought the tracks had just melted out to this enormous size by the warm temperature, but then I saw an eight-foot willow, just slightly bent over, and the tips of some of the highest branches were distinctly clipped off in clean, crisp hare fashion. Now, of course, the tree might have just sprung up from the melting snow. . .

March 16, 14°
        Q.: Bewildered by winter-spring fever?
        A.: Be wilder!

March 18, 7°   Fresh litter at the red squirrel's midden today. The warm temperature encourages more picnicking. Recently discarded shards of spruce cones pile high on top of the last snow. This brown debris will insulate the snow beneath, creating four-foot peaks that will remain long into spring, after the surrounding snow has melted. The winter relics are growing now, and I am amazed at the seemingly endless supply of spruce cones the squirrel has harvested. (Biologists say that red squirrels in the most productive territories may store up to a three-year supply of cones. This cache holds them over during poor cone production years.) An occasional dried mushroom is still visible tucked away in the branches, but most of these treasures have disappeared over the past months. The squirrel must be eager for the new crop.

March 19, 2°   Mystery tracks alongside the dog trail have me baffled. The tracks look like someone rode a unicycle through the snow, the pedals hit the ground with every revolution, and both pedals revolved at the same time. The only problem with this idea is that the creature was less than three feet tall, because it swerved under branches and bent-over trees without disturbing the snow-load. Perhaps a coyote or fox loping along, dragging a grouse in its jaws. I'm baffled.

March 21, 5°   *Spring Equinox.* To celebrate the season we take the dog teams over the ridge to Minto Flats. The country there is windy and open and you can see mountains to the north only 30 miles away. On the big lakes the wind has found room to remember the sea. Frozen water that will not whip into waves is scoured clean, and the whirl-away snow is packed hard along the east shore in drifts, reminding me of the arctic ice pack. On the windswept ice the sled dogs trot easily, their toenails tap-dancing along to give them footing. Cracks in the ice, air bubbles suspended for the winter, and the under-ice vegetation worry the pups at first, but they soon relax. The sled skitters around on the smooth ice and the brake is useless.

Ringing the ice is an edge of dark, frozen ooze, left exposed when last autumn's high water drained into the depths of the flats. The winds have swept away the snow, and on warmer days recently, the dark color of the ooze, slanting toward the sun on the north bank, has probably held a little solar heat. Marsh plants growing along the ooze still hold many ripe seeds.

Suddenly the dogs take chase after a band of small birds! Bright white patches on the seven or eight brown birds are startling against the dark ooze background, and for an instant I can't identify them. But, of course! They are snow buntings, the very first spring migrants that return north, a full month before any others. The buntings seem nervous as they land in a group of rushes, only to swoop off to another in less than a minute. They follow the band of dark ooze and vegetation, the lake's promise of springtime. The singing, swirling snow buntings form a band themselves, ever vibrating and pulsing north. This is the avian promise, beginning fulfillment of yet another season.

John and I consider this snow bunting encounter on the Spring Equinox to be a perfect celebration. The day is held by a gray sky, and tracing the sun's arc is impossible. But the curve of these small wings beating north is part of the same circle, and we are content. We share a picnic lunch, enjoying the last of the lowbush cranberries in muffins. There on the edge of the lake, the wind at our backs, we sit on the dogsled, turned on its side. The wind steals our body heat within ten minutes, and we down our hot bullion quickly. A huge flock of snowflakes beats in from the southwest. Soon this flock will overtake the snow buntings, and they will become one. The bright white wing patches will disappear, but the rusty-brown bodies will carry spring north.

Nothing can stop spring — not a gray sky hiding the sun, nor a thick blizzard hiding the first spring birds.

Mar. 22, 8°   The track mystery is solved. When John was in town he described the unicycle track to Bill Lentsch, a bush-pilot friend of ours. Bill knew exactly what John asked about. He'd seen the same thing from the air and followed the trail where it traipsed here and there and just about everywhere across Alaska. Everywhere, that is, where there are trees nearby. "Simple," Bill smiled: "porcupine!"

And sure enough, a few days later, down the trail 25 feet in front of my dog team, a small porky waddles for all he's worth toward the closest tree. The long golden hair is erect, as well as the back and tail full of quills. Luckily for my lead dogs and the porcupine, the nimble rodent shinnies up the trunk a few feet ahead of my dogs, who are earthbound by their connection to the rest of the team. From year to year I have seen trees with the bark chewed off in patches where porcupines have dined. Most of the trees survive, but occasionally a tree is girdled completely and the liquids cannot flow up to the leaves. Those trees die after several years. The porkies seem to prefer spruce, mostly white spruce. Of course, they nibble on birch once in a while, as well as on any wooden handle left in reach. In the latter case they must be attracted to the salt that has remained there from a sweaty grip.

One May I heard a porcupine humming up in a willow. He (I believe it was a male) started on one note and then raised the pitch after a minute or so. I found imitating his hum easy, and to my surprise, the porky responded to my version and started to come down out of his willow and move toward me. On closer inspection, he changed his mind and returned to his willow buds and his humming. Now whenever I come upon a porky in the woods, I try humming to it. Usually the creature listens my way for half a minute and then scrambles off. So much for my humming.

"The Guide to Wildlife Viewing," by the Department of Fish and Game's Non-Game Program, reports that porcupine bear their young in March. This must be just in time to get in shape for summer tree climbing, a little headstart on their predators, whose young will be born a little later.

March 23, 11°   Tonight the aurora chases around the sky again. Mostly sprays of yellow-green, fanning out from an unknown hand, and every so often a ribbon of pink, flung high to unravel as fast as my eyes can follow, faster than my head can swivel. I've heard the scientific explanation for auroras, but I prefer to create my own. A new theory every time I witness this wonder. One night I may see a Spanish dancer, whirling her ruffled skirt. Another night there may be a great ocean of iridescent plankton aflood in the sky, and still another night my favorite music has been transformed from sound to color and movement. Auroras are endless inspiration.

March 24, 15°   Today I venture over to my favorite knoll on the other side of the creek. I settle in a dry spot under a spruce and sit quietly. About a half hour later a gray jay joins me, sitting in some dry leaves under another tree about seven feet away. The jay fluffs up all of its feathers and then sings a

82

steady ten- to 15-minute serenade. I'm not sure the bird has noticed my presence. Jay looks so relaxed. After the singing is done, the bird systematically preens its feathers, working each tract of feather carefully, burying its beak deep in its breast, wing, and tail feathers. Next Jay scratches behind its eye with a sharp foot, just like the sled dogs do. I move to a more comfortable position, and Jay looks directly at me. I'm sure it has been aware of my presence all the while. How I enjoyed this private serenade and preening demonstration!

March 25, 17°   Moose are passing through this valley again. Perhaps the pregnant cows are drawn to the mineral lick in the next drainage to the south. Later in May or June, after they give birth, the cows will visit it frequently, pawing in the ooze, churning the muck until the ground water turns chalky white. I'm not sure what minerals are provided there, but at home the flying squirrels are gnawing on the moose-antler feeder. Over the years they have whittled down three of the pointed tines, gleaning calcium, I suspect. Perhaps the cows need this also, to aid bone formation in their fetuses.

The tracks and moose beds indicate at least three different moose, one with twins still beside her. If this cow is pregnant again, her interest in these almost-yearlings must be waning. After giving birth she will not tolerate them near her.

March 26, 18°   On the snow around the dried yarrow plants, delicate tracks of redpolls weave intricate patterns. The tall, warm, rust-colored yarrow offers hundreds of these brown seeds, which are scattered about by the redpolls. These lacy tracks are the winter snowflowers of the yarrow stems.

March 28, 15°   John surprises me with a downy great-horned owl feather he found on the snow. In the past they have roosted in our woodshed and on the porch of the cache, leaving feathers and pellets of fur and bone as calling cards. The female owl must be sitting on her eggs now, high up in a sturdy stick nest in the branches of an old tree, away off in some secret place in the far forest. Her mate hunts the burn, hooting out the hares and carrying them home to his hungry partner. Any day the eggs may hatch.

March 30, 25°   About midmorning a few specks of snow drift down from the dark sky. By 10:30 the air is totally white with gigantic crystals, no longer hesitant, but now determined to reach ground to add a few more inches of almost-ice.

I bake bread, put a pot of moose stew to simmer on the cookstove, and enjoy reorganizing the winter's accumulation of boxes, baskets, and bags on the loft. The suet on the bird feeders is buried by snow before lunch. This snowstorm should not surprise me; after all, the season is winter-spring. The temperature rises throughout the afternoon, teasing the 32° mark for the first time in many months.

Around two o'clock the snow stops, the clouds break up, and the temperature drops. Perhaps tomorrow's morning will again be cold and clear. Today this winter remembrance is welcomed. The new snow is gentle on the earth.

March 31, 24°   On the steep south-facing slopes, where the sun's angle is high, a thin crust is forming. On the level my snowshoes still settle a few inches before catching my weight. Under the big spruce, the ground is snow-free and the warm colors look inviting. Snowshoe hare tracks lead in under the branches. The hares must be kicking up their heels as the breeding season begins. I wonder if they wonder about the green shoots waiting to push up through the dead leaves. Spring is just around the sun a short way.

  The tracks that follow me also celebrate the joy of a new day, and, always, the small wonders of the year round Alaska.

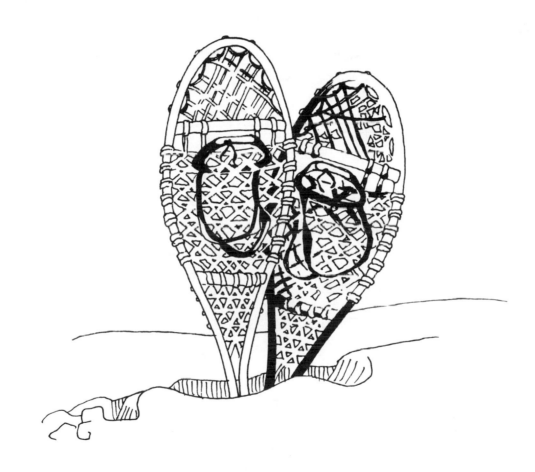